THE BOUTIQUE STUDIO BLUEPRINT

THE BOUTIQUE STUDIO BLUEPRINT

HOW TO OPEN AND OPERATE A SUCCESSFUL PERSONAL TRAINING STUDIO

DOUGLAS SHEPPARD

To Judy, Skye and Roxy.
You guys inspire me to be better every day.

CONTENTS

PART FOUR

WHO THIS BOOK IS FOR AND HOW TO USE IT

I birthed this book from a personal need. My passion to help others has satisfied my thirst to get a little better every day for over thirty years. The endorphin fueled rush I received from coaching would eventually carry over into mentoring and leading my team. The gratification I received as an owner who operated a viable business motivated me to write this book. I wanted to share the insights I learned from operating a boutique studio. As a business owner, it's easy to fall prey to the trap of being reactive and forget the source of our daily inspiration. I enjoy bringing people behind the velvet rope and providing access. I am motivated by helping others to achieve what they once thought unreachable. Running a successful gym does not have to be a secret. It's more achievable than some like to let on maintaining the correct action steps. Once I committed to opening a facility, I felt the need to gather as much information as possible on the subject. This included collecting many of the basic small business questions that need to be answered, such as who my consumer would be and how would I differentiate myself from my competitors in the saturated field of training gyms. I would also need to learn, on the fly, the importance of company culture and how to hire effectively. Now that my business would grow from a free-lancer business to a traditional brick and mortar small business startup, I needed to get an understanding of finances. How much money would I need and how long would it last? Outside of the banks, where could I get financing? As a service business, what was my product? Armed with the internet, I sought to find a book or books that answered these questions and more. It let me down to find out that there was not much under the fitness banner to help me. Yes, I could find marketing books that provided tips on attracting leads and prospective members, and there were a few motivational books to help keep me inspired, but once I would gain the customer, then what?

After cultivating an excellent product, building a team to carry out the process, and stimulating a culture that would ensure continued growth, I decided it was a good time to share my experiences so others could benefit. Then 2020 happened, bringing the COVID-19 and the global pandemic. This would put a test to my business like no other, and if my business survived, it would validate that I had built something more than a trend. If there is a single word that has been over-used throughout the pandemic, it's unprecedented. There wasn't a playbook or past case scenario any business owner could reference on how to manage their operations during the crisis. I share my experience and how I dealt with the pandemic.

Navigating through one of the most challenging times in the global economy, I was rewarded with having a business that not only survived, but could flourish post COVID-19. Included in this book are tactics I used to regain traction with pre-COVID numbers within one year.

I broke the book into four sections. Part One is my story and how I learned competency as a strength and conditioning coach. It isn't a memoir, but rather my journey and development as a free-lance worker. It also discusses how I learned when to dig in and when to cut my losses. Part Two asks the questions you must answer and breaks down the steps that should be taken and addressed prior to opening. What are you going to sell? How big is your operation going to be and how much cash do you need to get started? It also discusses how to get people to say yes. I will share our successful sales process and how it has changed little throughout the years. Part Three is for systems and operations and their importance. Most gyms and studios cannot afford and don't have the luxury of having a Chief Financial Officer (CFO) on staff. Understanding financials is critical for the longevity of any business. I explain the difference between good and bad debt. How to create your own set of key performance indicators (KPI) that will provide you with critical data and will help you keep score. This is where the value of pricing and capital reinvestment are discussed and their importance. I dedicated Part Four to hiring, employee development, and leadership. Many start-ups fail because they undervalue the importance of hiring good people. Many trainers and coaches don't come from a human resources background and relegate this step to hiring people who like to work out. Once you determine who is a good hire, you must accept the role to train them. I share how this is where you build the culture that will permeate your customers and members. I will share how we created something special, but also avoided a few costly mistakes along the way. Throughout the book I have highlighted valuable information into 27 Paradigms. These principals summarize key take-aways.

Scott Adams, creator of the Dilbert cartoon strip, has shared how it is incredibly challenging to be number one in any prospective field. An example of this is attempting to supplant Michael Jordan as the best basketball player of all time. The likelihood of you reaching this goal is improbable. Adams gives insight that as you add more categories to your goal as a filter, it helps to make the goal more attainable. It was this valuable insight I quickly embraced. In 2014, I had twenty-three years of experience as a personal trainer and understood the importance of leadership in opening a business that had over one employee. I also knew that the proficiency of being a solid operator would be a key to my success. My goal was to be in the top 5% of high skilled personal trainers who were also successful studio operators.

Now I would be mis-leading if I didn't state I've been overzealous and naïve in my journey. In this book, I will share the missteps and errors I've experienced along the way. Some of my most valuable lessons have come from the outcomes of these lapses in judgment. The significance is that these mistakes were not fatal to the existence of my business, and I was able to correct the fault and learn from them.

This book is a case study in how I opened and continue to operate a boutique training studio. I discuss the methods used and obstacles I experienced along the way. The case study method of business has been a successful and widely used process of teaching at higher learning institutions for years. Each business contains many variables and circumstances, such as timing, that play a large role in their success or failure.

I wrote this book as a template for the few, not the many. I hope it acts as an outline and reference for those looking to achieve success in operating a boutique gym. Thank you for purchasing it and enjoy the read.

PART ONE

CHAPTER 1

MY PERSPECTIVE

Per·spec·tive (Noun) A particular attitude toward or way of regarding something; a point of view:

I THINK it's important that you have an overview of how I got into the fitness industry. It will allow you to understand my perspective. We all possess biases based on life experiences. Your awareness of mine will allow you to understand the decisions and direction that I chose to take along my journey. There is not one sole path to achieve success, but many. There are various ways to operate a gym. I've learned how to be a competent operator of a training studio by not only observing other gyms, but also by learning from other industries. An example of one of those industries is restaurants. There are multiple similarities between the two industries. An experienced personal trainer can believe their experience in coaching will provide enough understanding to open a studio, like a chef opening a restaurant. Both strive to offer more than a product, but an experience. There is not a defined route to achieve competency as a chef. You could attend a culinary institute, apprentice in well-recognized restaurants, or learn while cooking in your own kitchen. As a trainer, you may have received an advanced degree in kinesiology or mentorship and worked alongside experienced coaches or learned through trial and error at the gym. Gyms and restaurants both have a front of the house (sales and operations) and a back of the house (preparation of food and the administration of the workout). What I've learned from restaurants is that you must have a good grasp on both. Delicious food or a quality workout will not overcome poor operations.

My experiences and different environments have a played a key role in the systems I have developed and chosen to use. Christopher Columbus and James Cook get credit for discovering America and Australia. Both countries were already there, but once both men saw them, they couldn't unsee them. Once I understood the role that anxiety and the fear of looking stupid affected a person's emotions initially when they entered a gym, I couldn't unsee that. I came to understand that people want to improve their fitness levels, like they want to be fed, but there are other underlying issues you will need to address. Gyms and restaurants are also social gatherings and sources of entertainment. Many gyms have members that continue to come without experiencing results, like people who frequent a restaurant for things outside of the food. Some people will choose to walk on a treadmill and others will order spaghetti and meatballs at an Italian restaurant. Just understand that there are a lot of ways to cook chicken and multiple ways to run a training studio.

IN THE BEGINNING

I was ten years old. My birthday was in a couple of weeks and my father asked me, "What do you want for your birthday?" I can honestly tell you he could not have expected what he heard next.

I had been thumbing through the pages of a consumers' distributing catalog. Consumers was a retail home goods chain store. I came across a pair of vinyl 10-pound dumbbells. That's what I wanted. I do not know what they retailed for back in 1980, but it must have been a good deal, because my father immediately told me we would go that weekend to purchase them. I've talked with my father over the years about this incident and how it would shape my love for lifting weights. Lifting weights in my formative years helped form a core value of exercising discipline. I wish I could tell you why I wanted them. Probably like most young kids, I felt that after a few weeks of using them, I would look like the superhero cartoons that I watched on TV.

Fast forward eleven years to 1991 and I was approaching a crossroads in life. I was twenty-one years old. I was attending Hofstra University in the evenings while working at Global Computer in the shipping department during the day. This is a time during my life when I could have benefited from mentorship. Part of the challenge was that the fitness industry was still in its infancy. There didn't exist a clear path for a professional trainer. I was attending a school for business administration. I chose that because I didn't think I could get a job with a liberal arts degree. Like many kids at that age, I was floundering. My parents had recently gotten divorced. I was living with my father, who was dealing with the financial scars of a messy divorce. His focus at the time was more on putting his life back together and not providing career guidance for his youngest son. I can understand that. I went through the motions at both work and school. The one thing that was consistent and fed my soul at the time was lifting weights.

Lifting weights had become my sanctuary. It helped me during high school as I played football and wrestled. It morphed into my new sport. Along with the physical benefits of exercise, it also became my reading interest. Initially, the draw was to look at the photos of the celebrated bodybuilders in the magazines, but after I finished gawking at the size of their pecs and biceps, I would read the training articles. I enjoyed learning about basic body mechanics and anatomy. I preferred referencing a muscle by the proper name as opposed to the common dialogue used in the gyms. Whether it was latissimus dorsi, vastus medialis, or posterior deltoid, I could not get enough of it. Then an opportunity came along that would change the trajectory of my life forever.

I had joined my first gym with my workout buddy, Jerry. We had met and partnered up at a local recreational center after deciding we wanted more from our workouts. Jerry saw I took my workouts seriously and that I was consistent. The value in having a training partner, outside of the benefit of a spotter, is the accountability. The closest gym was a fifteen-minute car ride, which created a slight dilemma for me because I did not have a car. Jerry would pick me up at 5:00 AM four days a week, and we would train early mornings together. Jerry was older than me by six years. He got a kick out of how I enjoyed reading about training and would talk nonstop about it. Jerry worked as a personal trainer at Bally's Total Fitness. Jerry would soon do one of the kindest acts anyone has ever done for me. One day, he asked me to meet him for lunch. At his job there was a small café. After arriving, Jerry nonchalantly introduced me to an associate of his. While waiting for my lunch order, this gentleman began asking me about training. It took little to get me started. This gentleman also noticed I enjoyed conversing with unfamiliar people and had an abundance of energy. I then remember him saying to Jerry, "You weren't exaggerating." Jerry nodded his head. The gentleman then said, "I've seen enough. Okay Jerry, you talk to him. If he wants the job, it's his." What job? Huh? I was confused.

The gym had been looking for a part-time personal trainer. The stranger's name was Bob, the area director for personal trainers. Jerry had mentioned to Bob I was a perfect fit. This lunch date was an impromptu interview.

I have reflected on my life's journey and if given the chance, there are few things I would do different. Many of the mistakes made have shaped me into who I am. If given the opportunity, I wish I made many of them sooner. The one thing I wish I did differently was how I handled college. I opted to leave school in my junior year. I was accumulating student loan debt and didn't have a plan or career path. People in the fitness sector were getting degrees in either physical education or kinesiology. They were directed to physical therapy school or becoming gym teachers. Neither of those routes attracted me. The attraction of sports performance training had not happened yet. I wish I would have stuck it out, garnering some type of degree which would have provided me with options later in life. Along with the fact I would have benefited, even if I could not appreciate, the continued formal education. There's also the discipline of getting your degree and finishing what you started. I opted to leave school and start working at Bally's in the evenings. My approach was that I would work two jobs for three months, and at the conclusion of the three months, I would decide which one I would keep full time. In hindsight, it's interesting that I assumed someone would eventually offer me a full-time job at Bally's. Maintaining both jobs minimized my risk.

This was an early example of how using calculated risk allowed me to move forward with a decision, using probability to determine possible long-term risk and loss. We romanticize taking risks. Living in Las Vegas, I've frequently observed this. The most I could lose was a little sleep and free time from working two jobs. The eventual upside was experiencing a trade that I fell in love with. When making business decisions, try to determine the maximum potential of both up and downside.

PARADIGM 1

Understand that nothing is 100%.
Use probability and calculated risk
to determine possible gains and losses.

Bally's Total Fitness was my first and only employer for training in my thirty plus year career. They did not supply me with any training or education for strength and conditioning, but they provided me with people to coach. New to training, experience was one of the best things I could have received. Bally's was my first step on my journey toward 10,000 hours. Adopting Malcolm Gladwell's Outlier's theory (mastery is gained after 10,000 hours of experience), I believe there is not a hack to gaining experience. Training is a science, and you are dealing with individuals. This was before screens and assessments. There were not any systems in place. Many of the strength and conditioning leaders were launching their own careers. The title strength coach was not part of dialogue yet. You had to get in the trenches and get in your reps training people. I tried different approaches. How much load to build strength? What was the difference between power and strength? How much rest between sets? How many days of the week could you train and continue to see results? These are the questions I contemplated. I observed what worked and what didn't and honed my craft to inspire and motivate people. During this time, I learned about empathy.

Looking back, I did a lot of things wrong. I pushed beginners too hard. I applied too much volume of work. I chose bad exercises. I can share this now, because back in the early 90s, we didn't know any better. Arnold Schwarzenegger escorted in the bodybuilding era. He authored an exercise encyclopedia that was widely sold. Conan, Rocky III, and Die Hard were box office hits in the movie theaters. Selectorized and muscle group training was accepted as credible. A stay-at-home spouse wants to lose twenty pounds, she was trained like Arnold. A senior citizen wants to get stronger; he was trained like Arnold. A thirty-year-old male, corporate executive, who has never been in a gym and wants to put on size, he was really trained like Arnold. However, along with making a lot of mistakes, I did a few things right.

I grew in my personal training as the strength and conditioning world matured. I initially embraced a bodybuilding (muscle hypertrophy) approach and then moved toward balance and functional (movement based) training. Along the way, I mixed in athletic and performance training (agility and power). All these influences happened because of either the introduction of a piece of equipment (stability ball, Bosu, TRX suspension trainer) or researched information. The late '90s and early 2000s became a time when the research world, based in kinesiology labs and departments of colleges and universities, challenged the validity of what coaches had been preaching as sacred law in the weight rooms. The National Strength and Conditioning Association (NSCA) was founded in 1978. This organization would soon start the publication of the Journal of Strength and Conditioning Research, a benchmark in the industry. I'm not ashamed to admit that I once thought performing exercises such as a press or squat on a stability ball were good drills. The research published would soon prove that strength benefits were compromised due to the overwhelming balance demands.[1] I would also learn that a drill is not deemed good simply because it's hard. You can jump in place for 45 minutes and you'll become out of breath and sweaty. I can't tell you if we improved your fitness level, mobility, or if done over time, that this would change your body composition.

After approximately five years of training people, I believed that there must be more in training. How do you differentiate yourself as a coach? In business, there is a saying that if you add -er as a suffix to a word in describing your business, your business is flawed. Examples are: "I'm better, nicer, bigger." To truly set yourself apart, you must offer something unique to the marketplace. I determined I wanted to absorb as much education as possible and combine an analytical approach with my high energy. In the late '90s, every coach used the same verbiage. "You got it, squeeze, two more reps." I also noticed that the exercise's focal points were the machines being used. The coaching was minimal. Once you adjusted the seat height on the machine and selected a load, the machine became the coach. I spent my time performing leg extensions and presses on the chest press, but I gradually started to gravitate more toward free weights based upon the opportunity to add variety. I preferred how the execution of the movement put ownership back on the coach for instruction.

PARADIGM 2

To gain traction in business, you must set yourself apart from competitors by being unique and different, not better. Offering something that is unique allows you to run in a race of one.

It's my opinion that the machine era of the '90s set many people up for future failure. If you wish to perform a seated leg extension, you only must consider a few variables. Once you have the proper seat adjustments, you need to select your load and you can begin executing repetitions until you reach your desired number. On day one, if you choose the right weight, you can achieve perfection. On the other end of the training spectrum, let's look at a lunge. One of the best, but also hardest, exercises to perform correctly. You must consider the differences in leg strength, mobility restrictions, core strength, and your ability to decelerate, and that's just the beginning. The correct approach may be to gain competency in other drills prior to attempting a lunge, but many attempt a lunge on day one. They struggle with their form and to complete ten repetitions. This is when the emotions of failure and regret can creep in. What we have learned in the strength and conditioning industry is that strength is a skill. It needs to be learned. If we take the approach similar to starting a new sport, that by applying the proper progressions you will improve over time with practice, you can combat many of the negative thoughts that accompany failure. Machines taught a generation that you can be perfect from the start. Why should I get off the leg press machine where I gain perfection, along with the positive dopamine fix to my brain? Why would I choose to struggle with performing lunges with that medicine ball?

Here's another part of the formula. If I could teach and communicate to the person how to perform the lunge, I would validate my coaching prowess, adding value to my services. It was obvious to me. They couldn't perform the movement prior to working with me, and now they could. I also thought of workouts with a more macro perspective. It was more than a single workout; it was a program. I would later learn how to use protocols such as periodization and the value of program design.

The next five years of my career would experience huge strides in personal and professional growth. I was gaining experience, learning exercise applications, and practicing my communication skills daily. The business of educating trainers and strength coaches grew from sheer demand. The fitness industry was booming. Gyms were popping up everywhere and growing in their size and dimension. As the size of facilities grew, so did the field of personal training. Because of the lack of licensing or regulation required, you had people transforming into trainers overnight with no form of education. Some entrepreneurs saw this surge in an unskilled workforce as an opportunity. Weekend conferences and certifications for the aspiring fitness professional were born. I benefited from many of these events. I attended classes and lectures from pioneers in the industry that taught the nuances of training.

It was an exciting time of learning. I learned new protocols and instantly applied and practiced. There was a lot of trial and error. The next pivotal lesson I learned was that it was not only my understanding of exercise, but what I could teach. Learning to communicate in a simple format was important. Regurgitating what I heard someone say would not be successful. I had to understand the concepts. This is where practice, again, served me well.

During this period, my skills improved. I never reached mastery and I believe that you never do. The road to mastery is a never-ending process. Investing time into your craft is similar to investing with money for a long-term benefit. The progress you make is too slow to notice. Morgan Housel stated in *The Psychology of Money*, "There are lots of overnight tragedies. There are rarely overnight miracles."[2] Understanding the process and the problems that occur helped to pay large dividends later when I would mentor and develop my team at the studio. As with any craft, users will experience periods of the infamous imposter syndrome. Imposter syndrome was popularized and gained attention from the 1978 research paper written by Pauline Rose Clance and Suzanne Imes.[3] A basic explanation is that when learning a new skill or craft, people commonly become overwhelmed by thoughts that they are a fraud. They have thoughts they are going to be found out at any moment. It can magnify those emotions in the fitness world. Part of attracting clientele is by sharing the story of how you can generate results. In the early phase of a trainer's career, lacking a slew of past clients, you are using practices and protocols from others. Lacking experience, you have not observed bringing a person through the journey. I can recall early in my career when I wondered, "Does this work?" I've read articles and research from others citing how, if I follow certain steps, it will. I used many of the strategies in my training and have experienced results. Were my results the standard?

Picture from Personal Training feature from New York Newsday, 2000.

Gaining the experience and the formation of a process on how I address someone looking for fat loss, muscle hypertrophy, or strength, and then seeing the process through, helped me to gain the needed confidence. I would lean on this confidence later to help drive sales at my studio. In sales, there are four *C's* that must exist. Each act as a step for the following. You first must have a competency of the skill, which then leads to confidence, which builds courage, to instill conviction in the user.

- **COMPETENCY**
- **CONFIDENCE**
- **COURAGE**
- **CONVICTION**

This is where the value of a mentor is clear. I share with young coaches that you cannot hack this process. There is no such thing as an overnight success. Show me a success and I'll show you a person who has been working tirelessly on their craft.

It was back in 1955 and Walt Disney had just opened his latest vision, Disneyland, in Anaheim, California. It was not a time that labor laws were strictly enforced. A young ten-year-old boy inquired about a job. They hired him to sell guidebooks for $0.50 each.

A year passed, and he was promoted to work in the magic shop. He played with humor and would practice jokes and simple prepared routines on customers of the shop. He soon realized that he loved entertaining others, specifically with comedy. He performed in small LA clubs as a teenager. His routines never lasted more than five minutes. He received no fanfare. He kept at it. As his confidence grew, so did the length of his routine. One to two minutes grew into five minutes and would eventually become a ten-minute act.

After another decade of learning and practicing, he took a job as a television writer. Through this job, he made connections and was able to get appearances on talk shows. By the mid-1970s, he had earned his way into being a consistent guest on The Tonight Show, starring Johnny Carson and Lorne Michael's hit show, Saturday Night Live.

Finally, after fifteen years of work, this man rose to fame. He toured throughout the United States and packed arenas. He sold 45,000 tickets for his three-day show in New York. He was considered one of America's top comedians and would later become one of the most successful of all time.

His name is Steve Martin.[4]

PARADIGM 3

Persistence and hard work will always beat talent in the long run. Put your time into mastering a craft and earning true competency. To speak on a subject matter with conviction, competency must be obtained first.

PART TWO

CHAPTER 2

WHO AM I GOING TO TRAIN?

THE FITNESS POPULATION is segmented into many demographics. You have the general population, sports performance and athletic training, youth training, training for seniors, pre- and post-natal training, to name a few. Each population has a designation on how to approach strength, power, mobility, and body composition. I dabbled in many of them, eventually deciding that I enjoyed working with the general population, improving body composition. A common career mistake is to be a trainer for everyone. Using a restaurant analogy, you wouldn't visit an Italian restaurant and ask them if they could prepare Pad Thai noodles, a popular Thai food dish. They may know how to do it and have a cook who knows how, but they would say no because it's not their specialty. My focus became how to stimulate and enhance fat loss while increasing strength for people over 40. I determined my ideal client was a male or female, over 40 looking to drop 25-30 pounds and improve strength. They were available to meet two-three days a week. I gravitated toward and enjoyed working with this demographic.

You don't have to select from the common list of demographics. You can create your own niche. A successful approach is to find a community not being served and serve them. Successful spin studio franchise, Soul Cycle, has cited that as the inspiration of their business model for years. Unless you are Walmart or Netflix, you can become financially successful, serving less than one thousand people. Create and lead your own tribe.

There is an emotional investment applied when training people. Every session is like a withdrawal from your emotional bank account. You need to work with people who will make emotional deposits to fill you back up. Constant withdrawals will lead to a negative bank account and burnout. Early in my career, my wife Judy and I administered a tennis performance clinic at a local state park. One of my clients ran a tennis program and felt many of his players could benefit from a workshop showing a few mobility and stability drills. At the completion of the workshop, as we packed up, I came across a gentleman in the parking lot who administered a youth soccer league. I saw him intermittently throughout the day as he worked on an adjoining field with his athletes. He had a lot of kids on the field. My quick observation was that it's a successful program. As I closed the trunk of my truck, I said to him in passing, "Looks like you had a good day." His response "I'm glad it's over, I can't stand kids." I walked away, confused. How could someone who had a distaste for kids operate a youth soccer program? That taught me an early lesson. You must enjoy the people you choose to service. You do have the option to select who you work with. All service businesses are a component of time. You can scale them, and in later chapters, I'll discuss how that developed into semi-private and team training, but the valuation of training is determined in time.

This is where apprenticeships have value. The Wikipedia definition of an apprenticeship is:

Apprenticeship is a system for training a new generation of practitioners of a trade or profession with on-the-job training and often some accompanying study (classroom work and reading). Apprenticeships can also enable practitioners to gain a license to practice in a regulated occupation. Most of their training is done while working for an employer who helps the apprentices learn their trade or profession, in exchange for their continued labor for an agreed period after they have achieved measurable competencies.

An apprenticeship provides the opportunity to learn a skill. It also exposes you to the environment of the trade. Part of that environment includes the demographic of whom you'll work with. Through a process of elimination, you can determine who you want to train by eliminating who you don't want to train. Each demographic will have their pros & cons, so I wouldn't recommend holding out for the perfect clientele. A simple exercise you can do is to ask yourself, if money was not an issue, and you were training people for free, who would you choose to work with? Books on happiness have discussed that many people take the initial approach once they enter the workforce to prioritize things in the order of: wealth, health, happiness. Many believe that once you achieve wealth, you can address your health, and you will become happy. I have observed that many that have achieved great levels of wealth are unhappy. By changing the order to happiness, health, and wealth, many people achieve wealth and improved health by making happiness their top priority. An indicator that you may not enjoy your work is by monitoring your mood.

If you work Monday through Friday and observe that your mood improves as you draw closer to the weekend, but it quickly diminishes by Sunday evening, that may be a sign. Part of improving as a coach requires you to hone your ability to communicate and manage the emotional intelligence of others. Mastering these skills demands hours of practice with people. Your mindset can affect the quality of your practice. Enjoying those you choose to work with can put you at an enhanced level of learning. This state of mind is flow state. Daniel Coyle, author of The Talent Code, discusses this in-depth in his book. His book shares a story about a six-minute video of a thirteen-year-old girl named Clarissa. The video shows Clarissa performing a daily practice session on her violin the day after her weekly lesson. The remarkable feat is that she achieves a month's worth of work in five minutes and forty-five seconds of practice. He calculates that her level of learning sped up by ten times. This affirms the theory that not all practice is the same, and there are variables that can manipulate the quality of learning. Your goal should be to optimize the environment of your learning.

Teaching involves communication and trust. You must get your point across, and the student needs to trust that what you are teaching is accurate. Relatability is part of this process. Understanding the mistakes someone may experience and explaining how to navigate through that process is important in the coaching/participant relationship. The ability to predict experiences pays dividends down the road. A good example of this is a female coach who has trained through multiple pregnancies, working with an expecting mother. Having children is not required to coach pre-natal woman, but it helps the process.

PARADIGM 4

All successful businesses operate on a system of applied skills. When establishing your business, determine the needed skillsets and optimize them within your system.

Once you establish who you want to train, you can dive into what is the outcome goal and the process of how you plan to train them. We can break the art of personal training into several sections. The more information you have on the participant, the better you can cater to their needs. In an era of data collection and its proven value, the takeaway is that once you identify what someone needs, your job is to give it to them.

A final key takeaway from determining who you are going to train is that this demographic will dictate the layout of your facility if you opt to open one. Once you establish your consumer, everything, which includes the marketing and how you provide the service, should cater to them. If you open a youth fitness studio, you'll need to commit floor space for a sitting area for the parents, because most of the kids you work with cannot drive or have access to a car. If you are in a city (New York, Chicago, Los Angeles) and a distance commute to work is the norm, your clientele are likely to train either before or after work. It's wise to consider space for locker rooms with shower facilities. This approach requires planning and time for thought, but it can save capital down the road, which in all business start-ups will determine your runway. It's important to note that 50% of all small businesses fail within five years[1]. Some of those reasons are due to lack of clarity of who their consumers are, or they deplete their capital reserves before their facility catches the flywheel affect and takes off. I can't stress enough the value of determining your *who* first because this will aid in many of the decisions you'll have to make.

FREE-LANCER VS. A BUSINESS

Up to this point, I have been sharing how to become a competent coach. This step is vital in operating a fitness facility. There have been successful facilities opened by people with a limited understanding of the service they provide. These are franchises, where part of the investment is the purchase of systems that are proven to work. The value of learning how to become an excellent coach is that you can eliminate that financial liability. In your business, decide which jobs you will take and which you will outsource. You will not have to hire a computer programmer to build a management software tool. For $200 a month, you can use the services of a company that already exists. In the fitness industry, program design and marketing are jobs you may opt to outsource. Consider the costs and contractual commitments.

When I opened, I chose not to outsource either program design or marketing because I had a thorough understanding of my consumer. The years and reps spent on the training floor provided valuable insight. I used surveys frequently to get insight and gain feedback. I asked for input from my fellow team members. This empowered us to attract customers and create an ideal experience. If a vendor attempts to tell you what your customer needs, that proves you have not invested enough time with your customer. If you have not opened a facility and do not have consumers, this goes back to the value of apprenticing or working for someone else. That time can provide insight into prospective consumers for you. Those years of working for someone else provide a platform for you to beta-test theories.

One of the early hurdles all competent trainers will reach is that once your schedule is full, you will see your financial ceiling slowly approaching. Personal training is a serviced based business where you charge someone for an allotment of time. Thirty minutes, forty-five minutes, one hour, or however you cut it, it's time and you have a limited resource of it. As you improve your credibility in your field, you will command a larger fee, and you can increase rates annually for cost-of-living adjustments, but there are market limitations to both. Life as a free-lancer is empowering. If you wish to make more money; you have the option to work more. This mindset launched an enormous economy known as the Gig Economy (UBER, DoorDash,

Airbnb). The ability to work flexible hours and when you want, was a source of inspiration for many coaches early on. The downside was that sick-time, vacation pay, and retirement plans were rarely, if ever, part of the equation. Learning the skills required to provide your service is important, but you should be able to clarify between a free-lancer and a business where you are leveraging the time of others.

If you are not looking to build a team and leverage the time of others, I strongly recommend you do not open a studio. You can achieve happiness as a free-lancer, and many have. The aim of opening a studio or gym is to scale. The revenue required to open a facility demands that. Along with long hours, you will need to build a team. Building that team will require you to develop and mentor people in a leadership position. There has never been a successful business that lacked leadership. If you know who you want to train, you understand the needs of your consumer, and you will build a team to service these people, you may be ready to open a facility. The time is never right, and you will never be one hundred percent ready. No one ever is. What you may have developed is the mindset that is required to operate a successful facility.

BUILD, MEASURE, LEARN

Step one is identifying who you are going to train. In this process, step two is figuring out their pain point or the problem you are going to solve for them. Early in my career, I observed how younger people didn't mind spending two hours in the gym, four to five days a week. As they got older and life became more complicated (job responsibilities, family needs, social demands, etc.), that time in the gym became a more valued commodity. The time to train became three, possibly two days a week, and for an hour. The time changed, but their goals and objectives didn't.

They still desired to lose body-fat and improve strength. I assessed that the efficiency of their workout became more important.

Whatever you determine as the needs of your clients, you must make them the focal point of their workout. The next step is to create a process of how you plan to deliver that workout. The workout may include a warm-up, tissue and mobility drills, movement preparatory exercises, strengthening exercises, and conditioning drills. You'll have to consider the order, the length, and the volume of exercises. This system will act as your template or framework for executing their workout. The small business startup frequently overlooked this step. What you must grasp is that eventually someone else will perform this task. Seasoned coaches struggle with this. You can't assume that the people you plan to hire will have your level of experience. I recommend you expect them to be an entry level practitioner. As your client base and business grow, you will need to expand your staff. That expansion may only include one other person, but it will be vital. Part of that process, which we'll discuss later, will be the onboarding and training of your team. To grow successfully, you will need to have coaches up to speed within the confinements of ninety days or fewer. A benefit of using a system is that your team will not have to do the creating, which can lead to an unexpected outcome. Proper program design is a hurdle and can have different interpretations. Using a system allows the user to execute. An added benefit is that the execution of your system will improve. This aligns with the premise that execution improves over time with practice. As an operator, you will value the ability to provide consistency in the delivery of your product. I can sum it up using a famous parable from Bruce Lee:

"I fear not the man who has practiced 10,000 kicks once, but I fear the man who has practiced one kick 10,000 times."

BRUCE LEE

The approach to this process has been the source of debate by many in the strength and conditioning world. On one side of the aisle, there are fans of utilizing forward thinking and innovative techniques in their training programs. These people lean toward high skill exercises, warm-ups, and protocols. On the opposing side, there are those who want a simplistic approach that is taught and scaled quickly. They focus more on basics and fundamentals. It's shopping at the farmers' market versus the large grocery chain. I think the best approach may be somewhere in the middle.

Early in my process, I determined I wanted to deliver a HIIT (high-intensity, interval, training) workout in a semi-private setting. The application of the workout allowed my ideal client to perform the workout two to three days a week and experience results. I used research [23] to help plan my protocols. I selected the suspension trainer, kettlebells, and sandbags as our core tools. These tools provided substantial exercise options (regressions and progressions), which would minimize user boredom. I determined that the maximum size of the training groups would be six participants. This number allowed us to deliver a high-level product in a small-group setting. The personalized feeling didn't evaporate within the small-group size. It developed a tribe like atmosphere among the users. I initially undervalued this bonding component.

Your goal is to create what we consider in the technology

world, a minimal viable product (MVP). This is a challenge for many early business owners. Accept that your initial product, the workout, will not be perfect. Trying to create perfection is something that keeps many people from ever putting forth a product. There is a saying that you get paid for what is done, not for perfection. Part of the process is getting users to use your product. Once they get to that point, you can collect feedback. This feedback loop is what will enable you to learn and start iterating to better suit their needs. To provide context, think about the first-generation iPhone. Many people forget they did not consider it an overwhelming success. There wasn't an app store. AT&T was the only carrier. There was poor reception, slow speed, and lack of memory. Steve Jobs and Apple were aware of this at the onset, but their goal was to get the iPhone in the hands of users, so they could start collecting data on how they wanted to use it. Once you craft how you plan to deliver your workout, a critical step will be to measure the data you collect.

PARADIGM 5

In delivery of a service or product, your initial goal is to create a feedback loop where you can consistently receive input from the end user which allows you to adjust and change. A feedback loop allows you to improve the experience and outcome for the user.

For years now, this process has been commonplace in Silicon Valley in many successful companies. You will constantly use the feedback from your users to innovate and create a better experience. Part of the process will be to adopt an approach that you are always working to improve your product. Like technology, the fitness industry is always changing. You need to consider how influences from society will affect your workouts. During my time in the industry, I have observed shifts from a bodybuilding approach to introducing balance and functional training to strength as the focal point. I believe someone coined the term that strong is the new skinny.

In the development of your workout, you need to identify the part of your plan that is an assumption. A couple of examples are the Sony Walkman and Peloton. Sony assumed people would listen to music in public. Peloton, an exercise equipment and media company, initially assumed people would cycle at home. In my scenario, I assumed people would train together in a small group within a studio setting. Semi-private training executed within a facility that had a smaller footprint was counterculture at the time compared to one-on-one private training performed within the confines of a traditional larger big-box gym. I didn't create semi-private training, but I wanted to execute the format in a studio less than 5,000 square feet. That approach increased my margins, decreased a hard cost, and minimized the risk of failure.

I learned the importance of clarifying the assumptions from a prior expensive lesson. In 2007, I attempted to launch a fitness software product. Apple had recently released the iPod and digitally-downloadable music was all the rage. Everyone wanted "1,000 songs in your pocket," as Steve Jobs had predicted. As a free-lance trainer, I thought the reason more people didn't exercise was because they didn't know how. That was my assumption. The current data told us that only 15% of our society had an active gym membership[4]. This was before social media and YouTube provided access to free instructional content. I started a company called iTrainer. We provided a database of over 600 downloadable instructional videos. The user could create a routine, just like creating a custom music playlist. MP3 player technology improved, and they started displaying video from MP4 files. My goal was to license this software to gym chains, allowing them to sell it to their membership base as a down-sell from personal training services. Two things happened. The iPhone came out, and the process changed from downloadable content to using an app directly on a smartphone. My bigger mistake was that my process did not include any level of accountability. I undervalued accountability.

Exhibiting iTrainer at the International Health and Racquet and Sports Club Association (IHRSA) conference

When I opened in 2015, people entered the studio looking for selectorized machines. It initially confused them to find suspension straps, kettlebells, and sandbags. They frequently asked me, "Can I get strong using these things?" Fast forward to the present, and functional tools are the norm in many training gyms. Taking this approach early on allowed me to differentiate from other competitors (Paradigm 2).

SIZE DOES MATTER

Understanding the "what" and "how" will allow you to determine the size of your facility. Leasing or possibly purchasing space, will be a challenge. Many businesses fall victim to failure because they commit to a space too large. The initial and somewhat naïve mindset is that you will need lots of space and you'll eventually grow into it. Space costs money. You have to consider that space is a hard cost and doesn't change, as the flow of business can. To avoid falling into this trap, what I did, and I recommend, is that you sublet initially. I consider this one reason how I could be profitable in my first year of business once I committed to a lease. Efficiency of your floor space should be a key goal when deciding how large to go.

Martial arts and dance studios are consistently good options to sublet from. They provide open floor space and traditionally have windows of down time available. This allows you to execute your system while undertaking minimal risk. I rented weekly floor space for a year from a ballroom dance studio as I beta-tested my semi-private training program. I could sell access to the sessions (this created cash flow), gain feedback, and learn from my early adopters. Once I established a base, it was appropriate for me to look for and commit to a space.

In *Crossing the Chasm*, Geoffrey Moore writes how the technology adoption life cycle is broken into five distinct groups. This concept can easily apply to the fitness world. He classifies these groups as the innovators, early adopters, early majority, late majority, and the laggards. [5]

In your situation, you are the innovator. You are solving the problem. In my situation, it was creating a HIIT workout administered by a coach, in a small-group setting, for fat loss and strength. The first group to try your product are the early adopters. They attract this group to things that are new and not discouraged by problems and glitches. Consider these the first people to purchase an iPhone. This group is typically small, but will be the providers of valuable feedback. In my situation, it was thirty people who took part in my semi-private training in a dance studio. They were okay using a kettlebell, suspension trainer, and sandbag (not the typical fitness tools seen in gyms at that time). The next group, early majority, consumes your product once you cross the moat, considered the chasm, and your product takes off. Many operators don't make it to this point, not realizing that the slow initial start is part of the process. Your product will experience enormous growth once you earn the trust of the early majority, as this group waits as you fix the initial bugs. In many industries, this is the peak of the growth curve. What you must understand is that it's the valuable feedback from the early adopters that will lead you to grow into the early majority. The next group is the late majority. The best example for this group is those that are forced to purchase an iPhone because they can only gain access to a service via an app. In the adoption life cycle, you see a decline once the late adopters appear. This shift is happening in the fitness industry, as people investigate joining boutique semi-private gyms instead of open access gyms. The fifth and final group are called the laggards. Those are people who never give the product a try.

In the initial stages of creating your workout, understand that curiosity will get people to try, but results and the experience will get them to stay. Eric Schmidt, former CEO and chair of Google, stated, "It's the product, it's the product, it's the product."[6] Your #1 priority is to improve your product. A better product is easier to sell. In a membership-based business, one of the top metrics you need to watch and track is retention. The quality of your workout and how it's delivered will determine your member retention. It is also better for economics to concentrate on that number. An accepted way of attracting new members is to purchase names and leads either through pay per click options online or lists for mailings. It's expensive and should not be a long-term strategy. It's less expensive to retain a member than to gain one. Over time, if done correctly, you should be able to lower marketing budgets for new member acquisitions. That revenue can be redistributed into member retention programs and promotions.

PARADIGM 6

Formulate a clear picture and be able to simply communicate exactly what your product is.

LOOKING FOR A SPACE

I'm not an expert in commercial real estate, but I will offer a simple bit of advice. Start small. You can always grow and get a larger space. It's favorable to bust at the seams, and this will also create a sense of demand within your consumer base. Having a waitlist to join is a better position than having a few people training within a large empty facility. A small space has limits and will hinder long-term growth, but if you are starting out and have not tested your product in the marketplace, this is a way to limit your exposure and liability. Space comes at a cost, and I recommend you start conservatively. When you are elbow to elbow with your coaches on your training floor and it is unsafe or you are turning prospects away because you cannot accommodate, you have then earned the right to open a discussion about expanding. The other question you need to answer is where to go. Where do you locate your studio? On this subject, I'll side with the experts that its location, location, location.

It's a better option to select a location where you have visibility than to opt for a larger footprint in the back of an industrial park. Many coaches have had to close because no one could find them. Select a location that you will not outgrow in two years. Operate and improve your product. Collect user data. If available, expand at the current location or move to a larger space at the four-to-five-year mark. Learning to operate in a smaller space will teach you how to maximize efficiency. Overhead is a hard cost and does not change. Lease expenses are part of your monthly burn rate. The lower your initial operating expenses, the longer your runway.

Leases are specific in each scenario. I would not recommend signing a lease for less than three years, or longer than five. The common lease is typically five years, with a five-year option. Many property owners will require a personal guarantee if you are not an established business. I recommend you avoid that, if possible. This is a discussion you will have to address with your legal counsel, which you should have. Keep the emotion out of selecting a location. I can remember the discussion I had with my attorney during the negotiations to renew our lease. It came down to if I was willing to move to save costs. I was once told by an experienced real estate developer, "You should never fall in love with wood and sheetrock." Your lease and payroll will be your largest liabilities. The difference is that you cannot adjust your lease based on the flow of business. Many of the titans within the fitness industry started at either a smaller or different location. The original Gold's Gym, made famous by Arnold Schwarzenegger in Pumping Iron, moved from their original 5,500 square foot location to their eventual 60,000 square foot home.

Money for tenet improvements (TI) and rent-free months

are all negotiable and every situation is unique. The commercial marketplace at the time you are searching is going to dictate much of what you can get in your lease. Hire a qualified attorney and have them review all documents with you. Laws and ordinances fluctuate from city to state. Ask questions and assume nothing. I've heard of trainers and coaches signing term sheets of leases without proper understanding of what they were signing. Understand that your gym can fail, and you should know all repercussions if you close prior to the end of your lease.

IT WAS ALL A DREAM

Up to this point, I have discussed who to train, the importance of how you'll perform this task, and where you may do it. To this point, the only investments you've had to make are time and energy. If you've sublet space to try out your widget, the risk and investment has been minimal. Now, as you go deeper into your venture, I'm going to recommend you pause and reflect on if you truly want to do this. Up to this point, it's been the adrenaline-fueled dream of opening your own studio or gym. This is what I've named the rainbows and unicorn phase. Everything is right in the universe, and nothing can go wrong. Then you wake up from your dream.

A lot is going to go wrong. You're going to make a lot of mistakes. Reading this book will not make you bullet-proof from error in your business. There isn't a book or mastermind group in the world that can provide that. Consider that many people attend Wharton and Stanford business schools in post-graduate work. They are learning from many of the best business minds in the world. Their studies include several case-studies of business that have both succeeded and failed. They attempt to start a business and fail. You need to consider that failure is a possibility.

Many small business owners can cite a specific time when they made the leap, and they experienced a paradigm shift. They looked at their business as a reality as opposed to a dream. It went from a "maybe" or "if," to a "when." This change in perspective fuels the entrepreneur to move forward and take action. I can specifically recall when this happened to me. It was after I returned from competing in a reality show. In 2013, Men's Health magazine enlarged their digital presence by creating a reality program online. They titled it "The Next Top Trainer." It was available on their website, and the concept was to recruit eight top trainers from around the United States that would compete in both mental and physical challenges. After each episode, a panel of fitness celebrities would eliminate a trainer and send them home. The show would air over eight episodes with a finale that would crown one trainer as America's Top Trainer. The prize was the chance to orchestrate and get featured in an exercise video that Men's Health would produce, promote, and sell. The reward leaned more toward media attention for the coach and less of a financial return. They considered their first year airing the program a success.

I entered the contest in 2014 after the inaugural year, on a whim. You had to load your bio along with a sample two-minute instructional video. The next step in the process was to promote your entry on all your social media platforms. Your friends and fans could vote for you by going to the Men's Health site. This was prior to America understanding the value of their data and privacy. I'm sure they placed cookies and other tracking means upon everyone that voted. After 30 days, the Men's Health digital team would determine who the top eight would be. I later learned that digital editor-in-chief, Adam Campbell, made the final decision on the entrees.

I made the cut and had to tell them within twenty-four hours if I wished to participate. I accepted the invitation. They planned to film eight episodes over a five-day window. My risk was minimal, and I figured it would be a fun experience. What I didn't expect was the impact it would have on my training and business career.

We filmed two episodes daily, and they eliminated a coach after each episode. I was the oldest participant (45 years of age), with the closest in age being fourteen years' difference. The judging leaned heavily upon looks and energy, and less upon knowledge and coaching experience. Up to this point in my career, I had focused all my energies on gaining competency as a coach. I had honed my communication skills. I had grown as a teacher. What I observed was fellow trainers in the industry, considered elite, were lacking in their understanding of body mechanics, basic anatomy, and exercise science. They all looked the part, but I questioned their grasp on teaching others.

Episode one of Men's Health "The Next Top Trainer"

I made it to the finale and earned third place. The show wrapped up the last day of shooting with a party among the film crew, judges, and a few from the Men's Health publication. I can remember being distracted with thoughts of how I wanted to lay out the floor plan of my studio. I was thinking of how I wanted to parlay this opportunity into a marketing campaign. My mind had shifted. I had gained confidence over the five days that provided me with the courage to make the jump. Nothing was guaranteed, and failure was a possibility. Many businesses fail because the owner eventually gives up, not because they lack traction. I was ready to test my fortitude as a studio operator.

In 1994, the Santa Clara Valley Historical Association privately interviewed Steve Jobs. In this interview, he shared one of his viewpoints on entrepreneurship. He stated that many people walk through life accepting the world the way it is. You're told to live life without "breaking too many things." He goes on to say that you can accept that dogma or realize that everything around you was created by other people no smarter than you. He considered that understanding as a pivotal life moment, and that if you accept that, you'll never look at things the same way. [7] This paradigm shift in thinking is critical to success as a sole operator. You need to believe that the current status is not the only way, and that you can make things better.

One challenge, among the many, is that some of your biggest naysayers will be the people who love you the most. Many successful entrepreneurs will tell you their parents, close friends, and spouses tried to talk them out of starting their business. This is from your support group!

PARADIGM 7

Know your why. Think about what opening a gym means to you. All businesses experience highs and lows. Understanding the motivation behind your driving force will help you to navigate through the inevitable challenges all business owners experience.

What you'll need to do is accept that there are going to be many sacrifices. It may take you years until you're profitable. You must define the cost of success and decide if you are prepared to pay the price. Nothing worthwhile is free. View time away from family and friends, the tough decisions, and perseverance as fees. These fees are the price you must pay to create something nice in exchange. It will take time to build a good team and during that building phase, team members will come and go. You'll be happy to see some go and then you'll have moments of despair when some of the good hires choose to leave. You will also miss some time at home. If you have a spouse and/or kids, this is a big consideration. If you refuse to miss any time away from family commitments, then opening a facility is not for you. I believe a time will come, if managed properly, you will regain some life balance, but not in the building phase. When you start a business, it's not only you. Your family and the people closest to you are involved. How so? They will need to accept that you only have a specific amount of time. There's a reason that new business owners pursue time-management books. I'll later discuss a successful time hack I have used for time management.

There are tactics and systems you can and should implement. Creating your model, testing it, improving your model, getting consumers to buy-in, and building your team are all things you must do. Using a franchise model is an option, but that costs money. You still must market your studio, sell memberships, and build a team. This is required from an entrepreneur. I have met people who thought opening a gym is not entrepreneurial. They are wrong.

Early on, I mentioned I rented space from a ballroom dancing instructor. The reason I had this opportunity was because his business was failing (and eventually closed). Prior to his closing, I started running small-group training sessions out of his place. One day, we had a casual discussion. He shared with me it discouraged him with the time he had to allocate working with his instructors. He told me he didn't want to be a babysitter. What he didn't understand was that people need to be led. If they had an abundance of initiative and expertise, they probably would not have agreed to work for him. He expected people to run his place like it was their own. That's possible, if you create a culture and mentor your staff. Expecting people to come in and run things how you would like it with no coaching isn't reality. This naïve mindset is common and is why he, and many start-ups, fail. I struggled early on with the time to handle minor problems. I felt I was consistently putting fires out. It wasn't until a successful restaurant and nightclub owner in Las Vegas told me, "That's your job." As the operator, you're constantly addressing the speed bumps and problems. Once I made that mind shift, I performed a better job.

Sean Parker, the founder of Napster and the first president of Facebook, has a great saying about what it's like to be an entrepreneur. "Being an entrepreneur is like chewing on glass, and you eventually start to enjoy the taste of your own blood." I share this quote as it's currently 2022, and the country is attempting to pull itself out of a global pandemic. Many gyms were closed permanently because of the COVID-19 outbreak. These were gyms that were running successfully prior to the pandemic. Hopefully, you don't have to operate during a pandemic, but things will happen that are out of your control. When Marc Andreessen, cofounder of Netscape (the startup that launched the internet era), responded to the question what's the most important piece of advice he could provide about starting a business, he responded by saying, "Don't do it." The meaning behind that response is that if you can be deterred that easily from what you are attempting to do, you should not open a business. Running a business is hard and you must accept that before you proceed any further, because now the liabilities and risk grow. It's been said that ignorance is bliss and not knowing the perils that are around the corner can be a benefit. If you knew everything involved, you wouldn't commit to it. My purpose here is to provide solid insight into things you should consider. Signing a lease agreement and hiring staff requires capital. A property owner and the people willing to work for you expect to be paid. That may require times when you can't afford to pay yourself. That's not shared on social media. Missing a family event because you need to cover one of your coaches, who is out sick, isn't inspirational, but it happens.

Like many businesses, my studio was closed by the Governor of Nevada in March 2020 because of the COVID-19 global pandemic. I placed the studio coaching staff on furlough. My operation's assistant continued working in a reduced role, to continue with back of the house tasks. The day I had to notify the coaches with the news was a bad day. I was distraught. There weren't many options and had to be done until I could figure out how to pivot. I immediately rented out equipment (kettlebells, sandbags, foam rollers) to the members and offered virtual sessions available six days a week. In the virtual setting, there is more demand put upon demonstration, so these workouts had a follow along approach. I performed each workout. Coaching three sessions, six days a week, was tough on my body, but I didn't see any other options. The goal here was to maintain cash flow, lower and cut expenses, and keep contact with the membership base. This was my version of offering takeout food, like the pivot many restaurants did during this time. My job now was to make sure once we came out of this, we were a viable business. This was about cutting all costs and trying to stay alive. One of my biggest fears was how my members would handle the behavior changes thrown upon them. If you are a coach, you are in the business of changing behavior. Coaches expel a lot of effort, motivating people to do things they don't want to do.

Overnight, my members didn't have my studio to walk into. The virtual sessions provided a way to maintain accountability with my members. I had people who had come through my doors four days a week for four years. I eventually reopened two months later, with restrictions, and could bring my team back. One year from the closing, we returned to pre-pandemic numbers. I share this not to boast, but to share my story about what being an entrepreneur can entail.

CHAPTER 3

SETTING UP THE FOUNDATION

THERE ARE GOING to be jobs initially you must do. It is economical to minimize the cost of paying someone to do some tasks. We've all seen the early pictures of Steve Jobs and Steve Bezos working out of their garages and offices. Not all jobs are the same. Some jobs require a specific skill set, and you are better off in those situations hiring a professional. This also minimizes the risks of doing things improperly. We all have that friend who attempts to do plumbing work in his home. He eventually hires a licensed plumber to fix the problem, plus the added things that were broken by trying to do the job himself. For your business, hire a certified public accountant (CPA). In setting up your company, you'll need someone skilled in accounting and tax practices to answer questions and prepare your returns. Tax laws vary from state to state and can change annually. Tax laws will determine how you choose to structure your business. Your accountant can act as a consultant if you need to raise or borrow capital. Gaining access to capital is not always a problem. The terms of the payback for the capital are the downfall of many start-ups. Aggressive, high interest rates coupled with short-term paybacks have put many operators in a hole which they can't climb out of. An experienced accountant can steer you clear of these poor choices and can advise you of better options. Some owners have attempted to perform the accountant duties. That's not a smart move. Your job is to build and grow your business, not to learn tax laws.

You will need to incorporate and form either an LLC (limited liability corporation) or corporation (S or C). Determining which is the best option for you is a discussion you should have with your accountant. In all decisions, you should be able to provide a reason "why" you did it. We form many decisions from a *monkey see; monkey do* mentality. The benefits of incorporating are that you instantly boost your credibility. You will protect both your brand and your personal assets. It provides tax flexibility and tax benefits. It allows you to deduct expenses related to the business. Ideally, you want to build something bigger than you. Incorporating provides the opportunity for your business to continue long past your time at the reins. Tax liabilities will determine which is going to be best for you, whether you form an LLC, C, or S corporation. Decide if the company is owned by individuals or shareholders. Each state regulates the laws governing corporations. Six of the top states for incorporating are:

- California
- Connecticut
- Delaware
- Maryland
- Nevada
- Pennsylvania

One thing that attracted me to Las Vegas was their small business friendly environment, low annual fees of incorporation, and lack of a state tax.

Keep your finances separate. You should have separate

checking accounts for your personal and business expenses. It's not good business practice to intermingle the two. Keeping them separate establishes financial clarity for bookkeeping and accounting purposes. I highly recommend you use a computer software such as QuickBooks to track all income and expenses. Most software will provide reports such as profit-and-loss statements, which will allow you to keep track of the financial health of your business. If you have challenges performing the bookkeeping entries, most accountants can either provide or refer a bookkeeper at a nominal fee.

You will need a credit card to perform purchases. It's a good practice to establish an excellent credit history through your company. Pay off charges monthly to limit paying additional fees from interest. If you must pay credit charges over time, pay them quickly to avoid the additional fees from interest. Choose credit cards with low interest rates. Many financial institutions and banks now offer introductory credit cards upon opening a business checking account. The offers will vary depending on the size of your business and your expected revenue projections. Remember, projections are exactly that, a projection. Most banks will want to see a history of past income. Establishing your company during your time as a free-lancer or sole proprietor will provide you with a history of past income. One of the best business relationships you can have is with your banker. Banks are in the business of lending money. They can be selective, and they can drag the borrowing process out. That's because they want to minimize their exposure and risk. Simply put, they want to get paid back. Understand their position; statistically 50% of all small business fail within the first five years. As you grow, your need for capital will grow. It helps to keep your banker abreast of upcoming plans (expansions, equipment purchases, additional locations, etc.). Banks devise different loan and credit programs all the time.

Start the process of building your business credit, and keeping your finances separate when you're a free-lancer. The earlier you start, the better your track record of cash flow and existence. The moment you receive income as a payment, incorporate. Many gym owners have conducted workouts in their garage, relegating incorporating until after they open a separate facility. Don't make that mistake. Early formulation of your LLC or corporation will become a positive benefit later when applying for credit lines and loans through banks.

> ## PARADIGM 8
> Take the necessary steps and pay the expense to set up the foundation of your business correctly.
> Don't treat your business like a hobby.

The number one reason businesses close is lack of capital. Their capital monthly burn rate exceeds their capital reserves. Debt is not a bad thing, but you need to understand how to manage and work with all liabilities. Bad debt is debt with high interest rates that has a fast payback. Borrowing capital that has credit card type interest rates and annual payback terms is a sure recipe for disaster. The gym business is not a software company. You will not experience growth that looks like a hockey stick on a growth chart. The gym business doesn't scale at the rate of technology companies. If done properly, growth will come at a steady pace. Many successful gyms that thrive today have succeeded at annual single digit growth rates. A key takeaway is that they followed one rule made famous by Berkshire Hathaway CEO, Warren Buffett. Buffett is arguably the best stock investor in the last fifty years.

"Rule Number One: Never lose money. Rule number two: Never forget Rule Number One."

WARREN BUFFETT

The capital in a training studio is the revenue collected from its members. There is a natural attrition that happens. Members will leave. Your goal should be to always gain more members than you lose in a monthly business. Using a compounding effect, you will experience consistent growth and a positive trajectory if you follow this principle.

Each month, you will have a base of expenses (BOE). This includes but is not limited to, your lease, payroll, utilities, the payback on any loans, and interest on those loans taken. Most businesses require eighteen months of operations until they become cash positive and generate enough monthly revenue to cover their monthly BOE. You must have enough capital reserve to cover all BOE during your initial growth phase. This is not a time to be conservative. It's better to have additional capital than not enough. This is where businesses may take high interest loans, which provides a short runway. Try to avoid this at all costs.

Raising revenue from friends and family is a smart and safe way to start. You can offer and negotiate fair payback rates, which provides you flexibility. I will later discuss management of debt in the financial section.

FIND A MENTOR

"Plans fail for lack of counsel, but with many advisers they succeed."

PROVERBS 15:22 (NIV)

Collecting insight from a trusted source is a valuable step in avoiding mistakes and errors. The key word in that statement is trusted. Listening to everyone and anyone is not a suitable method for how to operate your business. One of the largest assets a mentor provides is their experience. A mentor is someone a little further down the journey than you but doesn't have to be older. You should not have to re-invent the wheel in every decision you make. A mentor will guide and lift you up. The life of a business owner can be lonely. A few words from a mentor can provide companionship.

Many people start out with a parent as a mentor. I can attest that my father has been a mentor for me throughout my life. A mentor may also be a past employer from a prior job. Many companies assign new and younger employees to a senior employee as a mentor. A mentor can come as a book. I have received mentorship from Abraham Lincoln, Martin Luther King Jr., and Tony Dungy by reading books either authored by or about them. Having someone as a mentor does not require you to know them personally. Legendary coach, John Wooden, didn't know the thousands of people who would later reference him as their mentor before he passed in 2010.

"There is much to be known, life is short, and life is not life without knowledge. It is therefore an excellent device to acquire knowledge from everybody. Thus, by the sweat of another's brow, you win the reputation of being an oracle."

BALTASAR GRACIAN, 1601- 1658

You may meet with your mentor once a week, once a quarter, or annually. We do not attain the value in the time spent. Part of having a mentor is respecting their time. If you have time with them, be prepared and have your questions ready. Offering to take them to lunch or coffee is a productive way to meet. Don't discount having someone as a sounding board for important decisions you are contemplating.

PARADIGM 9

Find a mentor. A mentor can share valuable insight, provide moral support and unbiased judgment in times of need. Learn to use the experience of others to help you avoid costly struggles.

YOUR BIGGEST ASSET

Time is your biggest asset. Once you give it up, you can never get it back. You may have heard the saying that a wealthy person never pleads for more money as they lie on their deathbed. It is more time for which they yearn. As you open and operate your facility, you will consistently fight for time. I recently entered "time management" into the search on the Barnes and Noble site. I got 1,343 results. Time management is a dilemma for all new business owners.

You're not initially aware of every issue that will require time. You haven't hired someone to do every job and you must be frugal with how you allocate payroll resources. All business owners perform duties early on that will eventually go to someone else. In these situations, create a timeline dictating when you plan to hire out these tasks. A simple way to perform this with a gym is to establish break points based upon membership size or revenue. 0- 50 Members, 51- 150, 150- 300, as an example. Once you determine the KPI for the average rate each member pays monthly/ annually, you can figure this out.

I recommend you hire an administrative assistant early on. A common mistake among coaches is to hire only personnel that generate revenue which contributes to the bottom line of gross revenue. Trainers are reluctant to hire any position other than a trainer. What they don't realize is that an administrative assistant can help to make your time more efficient by handling many of the administrative responsibilities that mount up. Like the restaurant industry, you need a solid back of house (kitchen and food preparation area), but don't ignore the value of the front of the house staff (hosts and staff for the dining room area).

Even with a competent assistant and coaching team, you will still find yourself challenged for time. You handle this by assigning each day of your work week a theme. This is a technique popularized by many of the CEOs of Silicon Valley. Jack Dorsey, cofounder of Twitter and CEO of Square, shared this tip in an INC magazine interview[1]. I don't question that running a Fortune 500 company can come saddled with massive time hurdles, so I can't imagine running two companies of that magnitude concurrently. When asked in this interview, Dorsey shared that by assigning each day a theme, he could navigate throughout his day without missing a beat. The sample breakdown he provided for his week was:

Monday: Management
Tuesday: Product
Wednesday: Marketing/communications and growth
Thursday: Developers and partnerships
Friday: Culture and recruiting

"There are interruptions all the time," Dorsey said. "But I can quickly deal with an interruption and know it's Tuesday—I have product meetings and I need to focus on product stuff. It also sets a good cadence for the rest of the company."

Peter Drucker, considered the dean of this country's business and management philosophies by the *Wall Street Journal*, wrote in *The Effective Executive*, "The answer to the question, "What needs to be done?' almost always contains more than one urgent task. But effective executives do not splinter themselves. They concentrate on one task, if at all possible." The approach by some business owners is to master multi-tasking. Research has proven that to be incorrect. The skill in question is the ability to handle executive function. Wikipedia defines executive function as:

Executive Function- a set of cognitive processes that are necessary for the cognitive control of behavior: selecting and successfully monitoring behaviors that facilitate the attainment of chosen goals. -Wikipedia

The switching between goals, rule activation, and checking the accuracy of impending responses is where delays and errors can occur. The more complex the task, the more time delay and increase in errors. A study from 1998[2] determined that each task switch might waste only 1/10th of a second, but if you do a lot of switching in a day, it can add up to a loss of 40% of your productivity.

A successful approach that I have adopted and still use with success today is:

Monday- Marketing
Tuesday- Financials
Wednesday- Operations
Thursday- Sales/ new member acquisition
Friday- Employee development

I call them marketing Mondays. I think about and schedule all social media posts for the week. This includes filming and photo time. I schedule time to write for my blog. If I'm updating or changing the studio website, I will do it on Mondays. I dedicate this day to creative work. Many of these tasks require time to sit and think, as opposed to execution. Having a sole day dedicated to creative tasks and marketing allows me to write an idea and then leave it. Having the space to leave it for a week allows it the valuable "marinating time." In this scenario, it's not procrastination. You need to give time for the formation of ideas.

I handle financial and financial related issues on Tuesdays. Analysis of numbers and financials force me to narrow my concentration and focus. I enjoy listening to music and podcasts when working in my home office. On Tuesdays, all music and podcasts are silenced. As explained in the research, a higher rate of error can occur when multitasking if one job requires more complex work. I consider the scrutiny of numbers as complex work. Examples of things that I relegate for Tuesday include, but not limited to, processing payroll, review of monthly expense report (including profit-and-loss statements), and the consideration of future purchases for the studio and or staff.

I dedicate Wednesdays to all things that are operations related. Program design is currently on my list of duties, so I'll draft and review workouts on Wednesdays. I will iterate and look at ways we can refine and improve our execution of workouts. Member experience dissection is part of operations. We script the dialogue used to greet and confirm a member's next visit. Wednesdays include thought time when introducing a new training modality, exercise, or piece of equipment.

I deal with our sales process on Thursdays. This includes reviewing the rate of closings, the number of leads, and the sources. We prioritize Thursday for scheduling prospects to join, but will use other days of the week, if needed. Sales wait for no one, and when a person has made the emotional commitment to join, we don't make them wait. The initial decision is usually emotional. The goal is that once they enter our system, we can change behavior and make the process of training a rational decision by installing internal triggers. Having a good grasp on your sales process will enable you to explain the process from inquiry to the purchase of their membership.

Day five has been instrumental in our growth. Many people will address the need to allocate time to their schedule for marketing and financials. If you have read or understand basic business management, you will value the importance of having systems in place. I experienced an up-tick in revenue once I embraced employee development. In order to scale a business, you must effectively leverage the time of other people. What I initially undervalued is the impact employee development would have on my business.

In a training centered business, there may be a specific person who attracts a person to walk through your door. In a well-run organization, there's a high likelihood that a person will never serve this person. I live in Las Vegas. We consider Steve Wynn one pioneer of the Las Vegas Strip. Many credit him for the expansion and evolution of the modern Las Vegas Strip as an international destination. Luxury and elegance are words used when describing a hotel property developed by Wynn. I truly doubt guests of Wynn' properties expect their meals prepared or to be entertained by Mr. Wynn. He has developed his team to follow through and execute his vision. Why should your studio be any different? The best way to take care of your customers is to provide the best in training for your staff.

Employee development can include time for one-on-one with staff. Reviewing how they are growing within our system. Mentorship is part of employee development. Anyone in a leadership role plays a pivotal position in helping those they lead how to navigate through the choppy waters of career and personal development. When employee development is ignored, dysfunction has a way of creeping into an organization.

Once you create your weekly schedule, you will instantly have a feeling of relief. Designated times to handle specific tasks create a blueprint for your week. This also provides a plan for when nuclear issues happen and take you off task. You will know where you should return your focus. I wish I could tell you that everyone and every incident should respect your schedule, but of course they won't. Situations will occur that you cannot schedule for another time. In a 1954 speech to the Second Assembly of the World Council of Churches, former U.S. President Dwight D. Eisenhower, who was quoting Dr J. Roscoe Miller, president of Northwestern University, said: "I have two kinds of problems: the urgent and the important. The urgent are not important, and the important are never urgent." [3] This "Eisenhower Principle" is how he organized his workload and priorities. Years later, the Time Management Matrix became popularized by Stephen Covey in his book *The 7 Habits of Highly Effective People.*

	URGENT	NOT URGENT
IMPORTANT	**QUADRANT 1** IMPORTANT AND URGENT	**QUADRANT 2** IMPORTANT BUT NOT URGENT
NOT IMPORTANT	**QUADRANT 3** URGENT BUT NOT IMPORTANT	**QUADRANT 4** NOT IMPORTANT AND NOT URGENT

The goal is avoiding items reaching quadrant one that are urgent/important. Using the matrix as a filter, the goal should be to spend a generous portion of your time in quadrant two, addressing and focusing on items that will grow to large outcomes. You should avoid wasting time activities, busy work, and trivial tasks which are in quadrant four. Assign jobs a category to help clarify where they belong. After a few weeks of this drill, you will learn to decipher their hierarchy in your matrix and then determine the time justified on the task.

> ## PARADIGM 10
> Learn how to effectively manage your time. Learn how to quickly determine which fire needs to be put out immediately and which fires can burn longer. As a leader and business owner, you will always have fires burning.

It was September 29, 1982. In the window of a few days, seven people died in the Chicago area, after taking cyanide laced Extra-strength Tylenol. Tylenol is a painkiller manufactured by Johnson and Johnson and was their best-selling product. Tylenol accounted for 17% of Johnson and Johnson's net income. The marketing experts predicted this terrible situation would destroy the brand and that they would never recover. However, only two months later, Tylenol was headed back to the drugstore shelves, this time in tamper-proof packaging and bolstered by a thorough and extensive media campaign. A year later, its share of the $1.2 billion analgesic market, which had plunged to 7% from 37% following the poisoning, had climbed back to 30%. How did this happen?

During this crisis, Johnson and Johnson Chair James Burke pulled all Tylenol from the shelves. Prior to this, a recall of this magnitude had never happened. The recall and then re-launch of the product cost over 100 million in 1982. Burke's decision-making and crisis management during this time has been heralded as one of the top examples of good leadership in corporate America. He was determined to make Americans feel safe using his products. Burke earned his hefty salary and company stock during the months he coordinated the recall. As an operator, you will have to handle endless decisions. Each decision will have a different weight on the scale of importance. In managing your time as a studio owner, decide which decisions should consume the bulk of your time.

HOW MUCH IS YOUR TIME WORTH?

Early in my training career, I could rattle an answer to this question quickly. I charged a specific amount for an hour of training and instruction. Once I opened the studio, as my responsibilities grew, so went the list of the jobs I had to do. How I could avoid getting overwhelmed was to determine what my time was now worth, as the owner and operator of the studio. I had to consider what was the value of sitting with a prospective member sharing our marketing story and how we could help her? If the woman eventually joined and became a member for four years, I would consider that a good return on my investment of my thirty minutes. How much was the twenty minutes' worth I spent having coffee with a physician, who would eventually refer his patients to our studio? How valuable was the time I spent drafting and writing the operation's manual my coaches would use as a reference for their coaching on the studio floor? These are the questions I had to answer and give thought. It took me a couple of years, but as my business matured, I got a better grasp on the jobs I had to handle and what their value was. This also helped in determining which jobs I would delegate. Determining your value will take time. You need to compile a list of responsibilities to establish this value.

HECK YES OR HECK NO

As an operator, you will need to determine which opportunities are worth pursuing. Knowing how much an hour of your time is worth is step one. The next step is to determine the maximum upside and downside. Speculate. Unless you have a crystal ball, you have no other option. Once you open a facility, keeping yourself busy will not be a problem. What you'll need to do is create a filtering system that enables you to determine which time-consuming tasks are worth pursuing and which opportunities you should decline. Most of the time, it will come down to the math.

A reason many people struggle with saying no is because they don't have a way to communicate it without fear of insult. There is a way to politely turn someone down without igniting a negative reaction. James Clear, author of *Atomic Habits*, said "Massive amounts of time and energy are wasted optimizing things that should be left undone. You have to be great at saying no." I want to share two opportunities that were presented to me. One I took advantage of and one I declined.

During my days as a free-lance trainer, I worked with a Las Vegas couple for over ten years. The gentleman was a successful developer. He had developed and eventually sold residential housing, commercial properties, and hotels in both California and Nevada. He invited me to be a part of one of his latest ventures. It was 2016, and luxury apartment complexes were in demand throughout the US. He was building a high-end luxury complex with 250 units. The attraction to these apartments is the amenities that come included. They were installing a salt-water pool, beach volley-ball courts, a sports bar, and yes, a gym. To set themselves apart, they wanted to feature credentialed and high skilled trainers in their gym for the residents.

He offered me the opportunity to staff and run the personal training operations. They would build the gym to my liking. They offered to give me the naming rights of the gym as a branding opportunity. My upside was the chance to have a second location, with zero development and build-out cost. The downside was that I would have to staff a coach there thirty to forty hours a week. Using data I could find, I determined that residential gyms typically experience less than 10% of usage by the residents. On a property with 400 residents, this equated to 40 people who would use the gym. That group would include your casual user, who wants to either walk on a treadmill or use an elliptical. A generous assumption is that 15% of those who use the gym would opt to hire a personal trainer.

400 Residents x 10% penetration rate = 40 residents who actively use gym

40 active users x 15% Residents who hire a trainer = 6 prospects for personal training

It reminded me of my early days at Bally's Total Fitness. Every prospect wanted to see the Olympic size pool on the tour. Less than 5% of the members ever used the pool. The math did not support the liability of running the operations. Payroll is typically your second highest liability in small business. In this situation, the payroll of one full-time coach would exceed the gross revenue collected from training. There was a low ceiling for growth. Only residents could use the gym, and many residents would already have a pre-existing gym membership somewhere else. The final and most crucial consideration was that I had just opened my studio. I was still in the building phase. Running an individual location successfully is challenging enough, but to consider managing a second location this early in the process had the makings of a disastrous ending. My "Heck, no!" decision was based on the probability that to make that location a success I would have to focus most of my attention toward the project.

As I mentioned, I was finalist for Men's Health magazine Next Top Trainer competition. It took me out of my comfort zone and bolstered my confidence, which I would later need in opening the studio. This experience also provided me a preview of a new type of coach that was emerging. Peloton, YouTube, and other apps were gaining market share that provided a coach a platform to train people in scale. Coaching to a video camera or your phone is a unique skill set compared to working directly with a person or group in front of you. This type of training lacks immediate participant engagement, but compensates with instruction, both visual and oratory. Entertainment value plays a larger role. The participant can decide after watching for a few seconds (compared to the typical forty-five minutes to an hour of a typical training session), if they will commit their time. Five years later, this format of training would become a dominant player during the global pandemic and gym closures from COVID-19 in 2020. In learning what you enjoy, you also learn what you don't enjoy. In this experience, I learned I enjoy getting direct feedback from the people I work with. One of my super-powers is interpreting user feedback and then adjusting it to make the experience more personalized. I would use the insight I gained from this "Heck, yes" moment as a cornerstone of my business model for personalized semi-private training.

Understanding the value of your time allows you to determine how much time you can spend toward community projects. Community projects are like purchasing stocks. They can pay dividends for years. Acknowledgment from your community as the local expert is very valuable. In 2004, my wife and I started a community 5K race. My goal was to create a community event that could raise money for a local charity. I used the exposure gained from the race to establish myself as a local fitness expert. In three years, the race grew from eighty people to over three hundred. We partnered with the city of Las Vegas, raised money for a good charity, received a proclamation from the city and formed a relationship with the local feed of Fox news of Las Vegas.

Pictured with Proclamation from Mayor Oscar Goodman
and the City of Las Vegas

Carlos Ghosn, once considered Japan's most famous CEO, was the CEO of both Nissan and French automaker, Renault. During his tenure as CEO, his speech writer for three years was John Harris. Harris shared that one of his goals was to complete any speech for Ghosn in four drafts. It was simple economics. Securities analysis once told Harris that the notional value of the CEO's value was between $150,000 to $250,000 an hour. Harris shared in a Harvard Business Review interview that he knew not to waste his time.[4]

PARADIGM 11

Understand that time is your most precious asset.

HOW DO YOU TALK TO PEOPLE?

As an operator, you need to communicate well. The settings and environments that you speak in will vary, each carrying weight with its outcome. They may include, but are not limited to:

- Coaching people in training sessions
- Mentoring and working with your coaches
- Speaking with a prospective new member
- Presenting at an industry event
- Discussions with a vendor or service provider
- Sharing your elevator pitch at a networking opportunity

Each one of these examples is unique and requires a demeanor specific to the party involved. As an operator, I had to learn how to shift my speaking skills based on the environment. The dialogue within a coaching setting is like a dance. There is give and take, and each person has the chance to lead. The speaking voice can take on a different tone. This may appear different to the tone or approach used when working with a team member. There may be a shift in energy. In contrast, the communication when dealing with a prospect is completely different. In that scenario, you may take the role of more active listening.

Your ability to speak with your fellow team members and

staff will be a block in the foundation of your studio. Your ability to lead sways on your ability to get your message across. Jack Welch, the famed past CEO of GM, once stated that as the CEO of your organization, you need to be the "Chief Meaning Officer." [5]You need to communicate what needs to be done, but also inspire at the same time. Your ability to speak will improve once you comprehend the weight of your words. There is an old tenet that you should ask yourself when hiring. Based upon the way you speak; would you work for yourself?

The big lesson that an operator and owner learn early on is that your staff will have different goals than you. The people that work alongside you will not have the same worries as you. Don't expect your team members to lose sleep over ways to build your brand. They don't look at expenses weighing the return on investment or ROI. They shouldn't. It's not their business. You want to empower your people to work as if the business is their own, but you can't look at them with a negative perspective, which can transcribe to how you speak to them, if they don't take on that trait.

Andrew Grove was the CEO of Intel. They credit him as the pioneer in the growth phase of Silicon Valley. Grove believed that as a manager of people, you should have two primary focuses. In his book, *High Output Management*, he stated that "All you can do to improve output of an employee is motivate and train." Translate that as skill and will. Your ability to behest others to perform tasks in a manner you approve will come down to how you speak to them.

The time you spend coaching members and on the training floor at your facility will vary based on your model, but I recommend you maintain some level of training in your practice. This will allow you to uphold your skills as a coach. One of the most valuable skills in coaching is communication. In coaching, it's not only what you know, but what you can teach. One of the early mistakes made by coaches is to regurgitate everything they learn to the people they train. That's usually fed by insecurity and lack of in-depth understanding. As you mature as a coach and grasp a better understanding of the science, you appreciate that the art of coaching comes down to simplicity. The ability to take a complex concept and make it sound simple. Concepts, such as less is more, will resonate with you. This is a learned skilled and requires coaching maturity. Understanding how to unclutter your coach speak is important. Your growth as a communicator will be parallel to your growth as a listener. Active listening or giving someone your undivided attention will help you speak better to their needs. An example of this is the prospective person who wants to join your facility to drop 20 pounds. In your consultation, you may share the training strategy you would recommend. Sharing the benefits of exercises such as kettlebell swings and pushing a weighted sled across turf is better than explaining the process of how you perform the drills.

When coaching, direct people toward benefits or end results by implementing the required process. Use outcome scenarios in your dialogue instead of exercises and drills. The objective is to get the person to embrace the process. Coach Mike Krzyzewski of Duke University is one of the best coaches of all time. In his tenure at Duke University, he won 5 NCAA division titles while coaching many of the NBA's greatest players. Kobe Bryant opted to go directly to the NBA and forgo his chance to play in college. In high school, Coach Krzyzewski heavily recruited him. The two would eventually work together when Krzyzewski coached the US Olympic team in 2008 and 2012. The coach later shared in an interview that what he admired so much about Kobe was his passion for practice and the process. Early in his development, Kobe connected to benefits, which for him was praise as a basketball player, through the process or practice.

Every time someone asks you what you do for a living is a marketing opportunity. Identify this as a chance to sell what you do. This is where your two-minute dialogue or elevator pitch can come in handy. Have this down cold and be able to share what you do without taking a breath. Understand that outside of your mother, no one wants to listen to your life's accomplishments. This is when brevity is the key. In this scenario, words are a true commodity, so don't waste them. Practice your elevator pitch. Learning how to say what you do in a relaxed manner in as few words as possible is valuable.

As an owner, you will experience a consistent flow of vendors pitching you the benefits of their products. They will use terms such as "improve member retention" and "lower member acquisition costs" to lure you in. Your goal should be to cut through the marketing words and find out what the product does and how it may benefit you. You should determine if it will work with your consumers because you should have a better grasp of your members than a vendor. Early on, I learned that no one knows my people better than me. There are common characteristics among people, but those will vary based upon demographics and psychographics. Things that are appealing to experienced lifters are not necessarily going entice a person new to training. Learn how to be brief and direct when conversing with vendors.

PARADIGM 12

Learn how to adjust your way of communicating based upon the audience.

PART THREE

CHAPTER 4

MONDAYS ARE FOR MARKETING

GYM OWNERS LEARN, out of necessity, the value of marketing. The problem is that many can't differentiate between advertisements and marketing. An ad in a magazine, with an undistinguished demographic model depicting a price for training sessions, is an advertisement. A weekly blog article that tells a story about how and who you train is marketing. Competing on price is a quick race to the bottom.

In 2008, Kevin Kelly, the executive editor of *Wired Magazine*, wrote an essay, One Thousand True Fans[1]. In this essay, he debunked the myth that to be successful in business, you need millions of fans. He wrote how if you can build a fan base of one thousand raving fans, you are likely to be successful. This thought-provoking article was revolutionary. It embraces the stance that you will not be a product for everyone. You should narrow your focus and build a relationship with your tribe of believers. Your tribe are the people who believe in what you do, how you do it, and will pay you to get it. These people want to know you, like you, and in the end, trust you. Marketing is building a level of trust among your people and never violating that vow. This is following the marketing rule that people will spend money on those they know, like, and trust. Allow your following to grow by sharing your story. That story will attract those interested in what you have to offer. Over time, those people will grow to trust you, and in return they will buy goods and services from you.

Years ago, marketing was easy, but expensive. You picked your outlet, whether ads in newspapers, radio, or television, and spent money. Radio cost more than newspaper and television costs more than radio. They proved that the more you spent, the more you received back in new customers. Radio produced top forty shows on the airwaves where they could plug in commercials. There was never a lack of advertisers. Television was determined to be such a producer of revenue that soap companies such as Ivory sponsored programs during the day, so they could then advertise during the intermissions in commercials. This was the creation of the daytime drama or soap opera. Cable TV came into existence, and the choices of channels grew. The additional channels diluted the commercial process, but it was still profitable. Then the internet happened.

The internet created this new way to share information. You could share information for free, called a blog. This was early on and mainly for the early adopters. The internet took attention away from TV and the radio. This left the poor newspaper for dead. Then a few people created ways you could share what you were doing with your friends online. This grew into social media. Something else to grab your attention.

Each one of these outlets grew, and with it came advertisements. We are constantly being sold to. Every few minutes, someone, somewhere, is trying to sell you something. It may be an email, a banner ad in Instagram, or a logo on someone's shirt at the coffee shoppe. These un-asked for ads are everywhere. They have become white noise for many of us. They all look similar, and our brains ignore them. Podcasts have created value by selling access to content without the ads.

Attempting to stand out is like trying to get a drink of water from a firehose. Standing out or above the fray in a world we've built is very challenging. We don't remember ads, but we remember stories. Marketing is about telling your story. The story should be about how you can fix a problem. The goal is when a person who has that problem decides they are in enough pain or discomfort and wants to rid themselves of that pain and they come to see you. Marketing is addressing someone's pain point.

Prior to opening my studio, I noticed that many of my female clients hired me because they felt safe. Many of them were new to weight training, so they carried anxiety about entering the traditional big-box gym. They didn't want to look stupid, and they didn't want to sustain an injury. Unaware, I standardized an approach that was simple to maintain. I met them at the skill level they were at and used assessments to determine what they could do. I made them comfortable by allowing them to experience success early on. You do this by performing the appropriate movements. I used humor to calm anxiety. Johnny Carson, past host of *The Tonight Show* for thirty years, became one of television's best-known personalities. He used his quick wit and ability to actively listen and put guests at ease, relaxing them during interviews on his show.

Marketing can be complex. A logo is a marketing tool. Marketing is what the facility layout and impression upon entering is. A website and how quickly it's found on Google or Bing is marketing. Your blog and how you write it is marketing. Your presence and how they perceive you in your community is marketing. The organizations you align yourself with is marketing. Your YouTube channel and all social media outlets are marketing. Joint ventures are marketing. Distribution of free giveaways and downloadable material for an email is marketing. Body-fat challenges and the type of contests you promote are marketing. Your podcast is marketing. Public speaking is marketing. Attempting to master all these opportunities is a sure way to overwhelm yourself. Multi-million-dollar organizations that have marketing budgets hire PR firms to manage these entities. As a small business, you most likely will not have the budget or time to address each of these. I'm not a marketing guru, nor will I attempt to act as one. I understand what marketing is and how I choose to use it. Submerging and mastering one outlet is what I recommend you do. Once you have that established, you've earned the right to move on and undertake another. Pick one and do a good job at it. I have used our blog as a primary marketing tool. It allows me to share our story and speak with my tribe of followers.

BUILDING YOUR FRANKENSTEIN ROBOT

Early on, I discussed how you must have an ideal client in mind when creating your workout. A mistake is to take the approach to be all things to all people. In the marketing classic, *Positioning*, by Al Ries and Jack Trout, they state, "Years ago, when there were a lot fewer brands and a lot less advertising, it made sense to try to appeal to everybody. To win in today's competitive environment, you have to go out and make friends, carve out a specific niche in the market. Even if you lose a few doing so."[2] In order to extrapolate, you should collect data from your clients. If you are a free-lance coach, I recommend you transfer and scale your current group of clients into an initial membership base. Start your collection of data of the obvious demographics of age, race, and gender. Expand into where they live and their income. The next goal should be to collect info on where they spend their recreational time. These will be the foundation for building your client base. The purpose of performing this exercise is to create a filter that all marketing decisions will sift through.

Clayton Christensen was a globally recognized professor, best-selling author, and speaker. His best-selling book, *The Innovator's Dilemma: When Technologies Cause Great Firms to Fail,* is considered one of the top six books ever written on business by The Economist. It was this book that earned him the nickname of the "Father of Disruptive Innovation." One of the more popular stories of Christensen is when McDonalds hired him to improve their milkshake sales.

McDonald's is a sophisticated organization, and they had collected a substantial amount of data about their customers who purchased milkshakes. In this story, Christensen and his team determined that in order to improve milkshake sales, they had to understand what the job of the milkshake is. This touched on more than demographics. This was one of the early and popular stories about psychographics. As defined by Wikipedia:

Psychographics is a qualitative method used to describe traits of humans on psychological attributes. They have applied psychographics to the study of personality, values, opinions, attitudes, interests, and lifestyles.

Christensen would explain that their demographics told them that 50% of all shakes were purchased between 6:30-8:30 AM and that it was the only item purchased. Through interviews with customers, they found out some had tried doughnuts in the past, but they couldn't eat only one. Some customers had purchased a bagel prior to the milkshake but considered it dry and had to put cream cheese on it. They found that a nuisance to do while driving. One consumer shared that they had purchased a Snickers Bar™ before opting for a milkshake and felt guilty afterward. Another shared that they had purchased a banana, but decided it didn't do a good job, because they could consume it too fast.

Christensen would go to declare that the milkshake purchase served a purpose, or as he would state, "performed a job." The 'job' that all these people were 'hiring the shake for' was not only to put something in their stomachs, but to keep them 'engaged with life' during their long, boring, traffic-laden commute to work.

In my data collection, I determined that my consumer was:

- 60% Female/ 40% Male
- 52 years or older
- Possessed a minimal understanding of exercise
- Held a senior position at their job, self-employed or retired.
- Had anxiety about looking stupid when attempting exercise
- Fearful of injury and considered high-intensity exercise as risky
- Enjoyed being in social environments
- Very coachable and put a high value on coaching
- Wanted to be held accountable
- Considered exercise as a key to maintaining discipline in life
- Expected to be celebrated for showing up and for maintaining consistency

Understanding my customer gave me insight on how to craft promotional campaigns and contests. I learned how to speak to them in my blogs and emails. Comprehending my consumer helped me to determine which inspirational quotes spoke to them and were appropriate to put on the walls of the studio.

SPEND TIME ON YOUR PRODUCT NOT THE LOGO

Your logo is important, but I would not recommend hiring a firm to create it out of the gate. I've come across gyms, which will spend months of time and money on a logo, and then relegate a few hours on the programs that operate in their gym. I've never known someone who hired a coach because of their logo. Your logo is part of your story. If you are building a story that appeals to seniors, a logo that uses a font similar to the font used in superhero movies may not work. It should complement your story. Simplicity is important. Understand that you can always change it.

Many of the largest companies in the US changed their logo after starting. Microsoft, VRBO, Wal-Mart, and Domino's pizza have all changed their initial logos. Steve Jobs and Steve Wozniak came up with the name of Apple for their company in 1976. It represented the illusion of forbidden fruit in the Garden of Eden. They believed that everyone should have access to discover and create with computers. Ronald Wayne drew the first logo in 1976 and shows Sir Isaac Newton under an apple tree.[3] That would change in 1977 when a designer created the Apple logo with a rainbow scheme that would be used until 1999.

PARADIGM 13

Strive to always make your product better.

THE LAYOUT CULTIVATES THE ENVIRONMENT

The layout of your facility should encapsulate your philosophy toward training. I grew up in gyms and wasn't uncomfortable with dark and dungy gyms. The message was that dark and dirty symbolized hard-core. The dirtier the gym was, the better the results. One gym I first joined had a basement. You walked downstairs into two interconnected weight rooms. Operating a dirty studio today is inexcusable. In a place where people are going to sweat daily, cleaning a few times a year won't do. The current standards of cleanliness have changed. Once I opened, I took the approach that the best way to have a clean place is to maintain a level of cleanliness. I performed these duties for the first few weeks, understanding that this wouldn't exceed 30 days. I then hired a cleaning company. Understanding the value of my time, I knew my time was better spent elsewhere, and that this was a good job to delegate.

When I was investigating locations, I chose a location with floor to ceiling windows which allowed for natural light. I used color in the layout. The rig in the center of the floor, the kettlebells, and the flooring all have light colors. Of all the senses, we use sight the most and I wanted to use that to my advantage. A 16-kilogram kettlebell weight is the same whether it's black cast iron or coated in red neoprene. I understood that my prospective members had anxiety and preconceived thoughts of what a gym should look like. I wanted to dispel that myth and showcase a different appearance for a novel experience.

Picture of the studio floor at J & D Fitness

Front desk, sitting areas, and check-in space are important. Consider the amount of real estate you want to dedicate to this. This will depend on the daily volume, age, and flow of people or throughput coming into your facility. Many boutique studios and facilities of 5,000 square feet can get away with minimal space designated for entry and front desk area. Real estate comes at a cost, and you need to justify every foot. If you are working with youth, you are going to need an area for parents to sit, because they will be the transportation for your members. A front desk or reception area can direct people upon entering. We are all trained to approach the front desk for service. Operating a facility that is less than 3,000 square feet, I took the approach that whoever is working on the gym floor would always greet whoever entered. We positioned a high-top table with chairs at our entryway for a greeting area. This allows us adequate room to collect guest or prospective information and briefly speak with walk-ins.

You should have a layout that appeals to how you plan to train your members. This may include an area for tissue and body work (foam rolling) leading into a warm-up or mobility area. Then, based upon your training protocol, you can have designated floor space. This is where the POD setup at many strength and conditioning facilities has become the norm. The POD setup may include, but not limited to, a power-rack with a pull-up attachment, a pair of adjustable dumbbells, adjustable bench, and a lifting platform. One POD can accommodate multiple users at once. This is ideal for team training. If you plan on coaching agility and speed drills, you'll opt for turf and open space. Cardiovascular equipment (rowers, bikes, ski-machines) is lightweight and mobile, which allows you to move them when not in use. This is valuable in a boutique setting and doesn't force you to designate an area for that exclusively. It's become common practice to bring this equipment out when needed.

What you want to consider is having a flow to how your members go through both your gym and workout. If you want them to perform foam rolling first, it doesn't make practical sense to have the rollers in the back of the gym. Locate them by the entrance, so they can enter and immediately begin rolling. A well-respected coach and successful operator once told me you should have a conveyor belt approach to your workout. People come in and get put through the process industrially. This doesn't belittle the value of your members, nor does it cite a lack of personalized attention. It simply states that there should be a system with a pragmatic approach. I couldn't agree more.

Setting up your facility around how you will conduct the workout also speaks to your consumer. It helps them to know what to expect. This is the power of franchises. When you walk into a Starbucks coffee shop, you have an expectation of what to expect. There is an area to order with the drink menu highly visible. They have a bar to pick up the prepared drinks. To the side are tables and chairs to sit and enjoy your beverage. If you frequent a shop like this, you become trained on how to order and where to get your drink. You want a similar experience for your members. Come in, warm-up, receive coaching, and leave.

LOW BARRIER TO ENTRY

One of the best marketing tactics you can implement is a trial membership. Trial memberships, or Front-end-offers (FEO) aren't new and have been used in various types of businesses models for a while. The idea of a trial offer is to offer someone the opportunity to try your service or product at a discounted rate and for a brief duration. There must be a price to establish value and it can't be for free. Why is this tactic effective and the "Try a Free Workout" flawed? Getting someone to come to your facility is more than a retail purchase. You are attempting to create a change in behavior by forming a habit. You are using the trial membership as an external trigger to stimulate the user to take action.

Action is critical to create a habit. Dr. B.J. Fogg, Director of the Persuasive Technology Lab at Stanford University, has theorized a model that acts as a way to understand what drives our actions. "Fogg posts that there are three ingredients required to initiate any and all behaviors: (1) the user must have sufficient motivation; (2) the user must have the ability to complete the desired action; and (3) a trigger must be present to activate the behavior."[4]

Providing an end date of less than 30-days provides a level of optimism of completion for the user. Creating a workout that the user can successfully complete grants a sufficient motivation and a positive emotion. The workouts during the trial must be challenging enough to maintain engagement, but not overly difficult, which can form emotions of failure and doubt. Once training at your facility becomes tightly partnered with a positive emotion and an existing routine, it forms an internal trigger. The desired outcome is that during the trial period, an internal trigger will replace the external trigger. The technology community has effectively used this approach for years. An example is downloading an app a friend recommends (external trigger). You use the app. Over a brief time span of three weeks, you routinely open and check the app without being prompted.

The key is to have the trial last long enough that the user experiences this shift in behavior and the experience at your gym forms the habit or "sticky," as referred to in marketing. This is one of the big differences between advertising and marketing.

In contrast, I wouldn't recommend you attempt to propel consumers to use your gym because it's the most inexpensive. In that scenario, price is the only variable you can manipulate. If a competitor challenges you on price, you will have no choice but to go lower. The race to the bottom soon follows. A trial membership lowers the initial risk for the user. It comes with only one caveat. In a trial membership, you must follow through on your promises.

ADVERTISEMENT SCENARIO

A woman receives an email from a "Deal of the Day" website. The price in the ad attracts and piques her interest. The motivational driver in the ad is price. This ad is selling access to a gym that specializes in fat loss workouts. The ad offers unlimited access for a month. She clicks and makes the purchase. There's an endorphin rush, and she immediately feels motivated by the purchase. She takes action to go the following day. On her first day, the trainer she meets never makes eye contact when speaking to her and has bad breath. She feels the workout is too hard and has anxiety that she may get hurt. The bathrooms are dirty, and the gym smells funny. None of the members speak to her. She loses enthusiasm after two weeks and stops going. She feels taken, and that it was a waste of her money. That weekend, she tells three of her friends about the unpleasant experience over cocktails.

MARKETING SCENARIO

On his way to work, a gentleman spots a banner on a building that reads, "Three weeks Unlimited Personal Training." He stops by on his way home to get more info. A staff member greets him when he enters and explains that it's a trial membership and costs $200. He signs up and gives it a try.

He comes in the following day. As he enters the facility, a member of the staff immediately greets him. The staff member introduces him to a few of the members, shows him where he can put his belongings, and then explains the format of the workout. He notices the gym is spotless. A coach conducts a quick assessment of him. The workout is challenging, but he feels energized, not beat down. The next day, he comes back. He meets another coach and experiences another great workout. He meets a few more members. After three weeks, he's been in nine times. At this point, he feels more disciplined in his daily decisions and, for example, turns down going for pizza with friends over the weekend. He loses five pounds in the three weeks. He talks about the gym at work and inspires a coworker to join with him.

Trial memberships can be the primary lead driver in a gym or studio. The objective is to have someone experience everything you offer. You want to convert a rational decision, their choice to try something with minimal risk exposure (time and financial) and convert it to an emotional decision. That emotion is how they feel and is the upside of continuing.

Considerations of your valuation for a new lead should be part of determining your price for the trial membership.

Conversion rates of trial members to full-time members and the average time a member stays at your gym will dictate how much you discount the trial. Here's an example:

You offer a trial membership of $299 for unlimited personal training and nutritional coaching for 21 days. You track and determine that you convert 75% of all trial members to full-time members. The average lifetime of your full-time members is 30 months, with an average monthly EFT (electronic fund transfer) membership of $299. That means you will collect $8,970 from that member over 2 ½ years.

A trial membership will act as a filter as you build your tribe. The people that appreciate what you offer and will pay to get it will probably find you through a trial.

WEBSITE DESIGN AND SEARCH ENGINE OPTIMIZATION

You will need to create a website. As the world has become mobile and most people walk around with a super-computer in their pocket, your website can act as a source of leads and new member generation. There are many companies available that will provide you with a template for the layout of your website. Gone are the days of when you had to start from scratch. You will not need to hire a programmer who can write code. Since the shift has gone to mobile, design a site that looks appealing on a smaller screen and on a desktop. The industry has grown so that we now have companies that create websites for specific industries. Investigate and find an organization that creates websites for fitness, strength, and conditioning organizations. It's important that the layout allows for content growth. Your website becomes an extension of your company. The platform should add updates to stay current. The look and feel of your website should align with your message and speak to your ideal member. Consistency is important.

A valuable tool you should include on your website is testimonials. People like to see what the consumer says about your product. This is the reason sites such as Yelp have become popular. Once you work with people, collect testimonials. The key is to make collecting the testimonials easy for your members. Eliminate any friction. Draft a few questions which you can send in an email and they can answer. This will become their testimonial. This will act as a template, so that the testimonials are consistent. An example is:

- Why did you join XYZ studio?
- What improvements have you made since joining XYZ studio?
- What do you like most about XYZ studio?

You want to create a website that will translate into a source of lead generation. This is the first impression of your studio and what it offers. It should provide who you are, what you offer (the problem you can fix), and proof that you can fulfill that promise. Offering a "Money-Back Guarantee" is helpful and is a way of mitigating risk away from the prospect. If you opt to include this marketing tool, in this respect, fulfill the obligation if someone requests their money back. Some companies offer this and then make it challenging for the consumer to get their money back. You should include photos of yourself and your staff. Have them professionally done. People like to see who they are going to hire. There are software tracking tools, such as heat mapping and free analytics available on search engines, which inform you where your users go once they reach your website. The benefit of using tools like this is that it makes it easier for you to learn from your users and build a better web design.

Your website is also your first opportunity for email collection. You should have an easily found opt in button that allows a visitor to submit their email to receive content from you. Part of marketing is email list building. This is how you strategically create your sales funnel. You are forming your audience. To entice and reward, you may include a form of free content (i.e., workout video, newsletter, eBook). This is where you start your story. Years ago, the eBook was a popular option, but as people have become enamored with free E-books, this has lost some of its luster. This is because eBooks are downloaded and filed away. People forget about them and never read them. Weekly newsletters have risen in favor. They require less of a time commitment. Building your email lists allows you to perform invite marketing. Invite marketing is not spam. Invite marketing is how you can communicate with your followers. This is your tribe and the people who have provided you their email in exchange to stay informed of what you are doing. Automate this task. Once you have the site created, the next step is the challenge. How will people find it?

Google is the number one source of search on the internet. There are self-proclaimed masters of search engine optimization (SEO). They state they can improve your rank in Google. The problem with that claim is that no one controls Google. Google changes the rules all the time by adjusting the search algorithm they use. Their algorithm acts as a filter for the internet. The Google algorithm positively weighs content and keywords you have on each page of your website. All content, including video content, become weighted. The more videos you have, the better your ranking on search. Posts on your social media, such as Instagram, and posts on your blog will all help. Engagement is important, so create content people want to see. It's important that you create content. A lot of content. We should not understate that the content needs to be good and search worthy. Sumner Redstone, former chair of Viacom CBS and media magnate, made famous the statement, that "content is king."

There are different routes which you can take determining what you create. There are tools you can use to find out high-ranking search items. The approach you should take is to be a big fish in a small pond, as opposed to being a tadpole in the ocean. In a report written by DOMO (Data Never Sleeps), "Over 2.5 quintillion bytes of data are created every single day and it's only going to grow from there. By 2020, it's estimated that 1.7MB of data will be created every second for every person on earth."[5]

What you need to determine is how you plan to be heard or watched. Use your strengths. If you are a competent writer, create a blog and use that as your platform. If you lean more toward public speaking, dedicate yourself to creating a podcast. You can create video content if you are comfortable in front of the camera. Pick one and consistently work to create quality content. Consider yourself like a film or series trying to be found on the Netflix's or Disney streaming services. Content is king, and consumers will find the more desirable content. Google considers content that receives high numbers of downloads and views as favorable and helps to promote by elevating the ranking status of highly sought-after content. You should track the response which you receive from your content. This allows you to cater to what your followers enjoy and want.

In my situation, I established my blog as the primary source for building followers and email collection. We created a schedule for posts and kept to it. I used the engagement from my readers and monitored the open and click through rate of the posts to determine my topics. I wrote about strength and conditioning insight, motivation, and the culture at the studio.

THE NUMBER ONE SOURCE OF LEADS

Word of mouth has traditionally been the number one source of getting prospects and leads in small business. Providing results for your members is the easiest and most cost-effective way to create a funnel of consistent leads. People enjoy talking about themselves. Sharing their relationship with your gym or studio and results achieved can be a popular topic of discussion. The key is to train your members as the front line of your sales team by sharing their story with others. Business owners will agree that word of mouth is their largest source of leads. Don't make the common error and take a random approach with it. The best way to get leads from your members is to ask. It isn't hard, but it should be strategic and anchored to specific emotional events to improve the rate of success.

When a person joins your gym, the anticipation sends a surge of dopamine to their brain. They haven't reached their goal, but they have started the process. This signals the peak of the clean slate mindset that they are about to make a change. You can capitalize on this by asking if they have anyone they could recommend that may also be interested in joining your gym. A key step is to associate the joining process with fixing a problem. It doesn't have to be the same problem they are experiencing, but that can act as an opening.

Example:

Coach/Salesperson- Mary, we're happy to have you on board and can't wait to help start your journey of dropping body-fat. Do you have any friends or family that have struggled with dropping body-fat that we could also help?

Mary- I have a friend at work that has been trying to drop 20 pounds for the last year.

Coach/Salesperson- I would like to help her. Would you be comfortable giving me her name and phone number so I could discuss how we can help?

Mary- Let me ask her if it's okay to give out her number.

Coach/ Salesperson- That's perfect. Here's my card you can give her. Here's a small card that you can write her name, email, and a good time I can reach her. If she agrees, please fill it out and bring it with you on your next visit.

This is permission marketing and avoids the cold-calling approach. Having a brief form that has the contact information also creates a source of tracking the lead.

Every time a member pays for services, it's an investment and reinforces the habit of using your services. That's an ideal time to offer an incentive for referring a prospective member. Emailed receipts are an excellent location to place an external trigger requesting a referral. The incentive may be a discount on their monthly dues once a referral they provide joins. Tracking the average ETF or monthly dues received from members and the average lift-time of each member provides you the needed data for determining how much you can spend on the discount. Here's an example:

If the average member spends $200 per month for services and has an average life span of two years at your studio, offering a discount of $100 is a good ROI. Using this method, you net $4,700.

$200 (avg. monthly ETF) x 24 months (avg. lifespan of members) – $4,800

$4,800 - $100 (discount given to member for referral) = $4,700

Another tactic to generate referrals from members is to have a contest. Prizes can range from discounts, added time to an existing membership and/or an apparel giveaway. Apparel prizes have a positive track record of motivating people to take part in referral contests. As stated in *Hooked: How to Build Habit-Forming Products*, by Nir Eyal, "Our brains are adapted to seek rewards that make us feel accepted, attractive, important, and included." Giving someone a sweatshirt branded with your studio name and logo satisfies that need. Contests don't require a lot of energy to promote and operate. To maintain a level of urgency, keep the length of the contest to a month or shorter.

PARADIGM 14

Use marketing as a vehicle to share your story. Your goal is to attract the people looking for what you have to offer.

Use marketing as a vehicle to share your story. Your goal is to attract the people looking for what you have to offer.

CHAPTER 5

BY THE NUMBERS

TO OPERATE A SUCCESSFUL TRAINING STUDIO, create a service that people want. The next step is to have a grasp of the financials and how to manage the cash flow which the business will generate. Cash flow is the life source of the business. The cash flow creates an ebb and flow which enables you to pay expenses and debts, business development, and reinvestment. Many small businesses spend the lifetime of the business walking on a tightrope balancing between keeping their doors open or shutting the doors for good. You should create a monthly cash flow statement, which will communicate how much cash is coming in and how much is going out. You must devote time to learning what the numbers mean. Once you gain competence in understanding your financials, you can create KPI which allow you to track trends. Creating a plan for prosperity is easy. Writing up numbers that end with a positive outcome is not a business, it's math. The summation of a successful sales system, a united team, and competent operations will make those numbers a reality.

You should have an accountant. It should not limit their role to only annual tax preparation. You should have frequent meetings (monthly or quarterly) to review financial reports and to lean on them for financial advisement. In the fitness world, it appears obvious when someone who doesn't understand or know how to achieve their fitness goal should seek help from a professional. That concept holds true when you're working and learning the financials of your business. Ask for help.

Revenue cycles for most gyms will revolve around a monthly cycle. The reason is that you should offer your product as a membership. Years ago, personal training was sold on a per session basis. Gyms sold personal training packages of 10, 20, 30 sessions and more. The problem with that approach was two-fold. It's hard to manage cash flow with moving receivables. Once I started selling semi-private training, I converted everyone to a monthly membership. This included private training. Using this model, you can avoid the cash flow deficit many small businesses fall into. You are using the revenue from your members to finance your business. The second and more alarming problem of selling sessions in lieu of monthly memberships is that many incentivized the lower price which generates a lower gross margin. The only way someone will give you more money up front is to make it less expensive. The more they purchase the cheaper it gets. The people who purchase the larger packages tend to stay with you the longest and are the most committed. By doing that, you just awarded your biggest fan with the lowest price. It should be the other way around. People who value what you have to offer don't mind paying more for services.

Predictions are a forecast on what you expect to happen. As you gain more experience, you will be more precise with your predictions, but initially there is a substantial amount of guessing coupled with optimism. That's fine and is to be expected in any startup operation. It's important that you don't confuse hope for a plan. You should be able to justify all numbers with an explanation. You don't want to be the Iowa farmer, who Kevin Costner portrays in the movie *Field of Dreams*, who believes he only needs to build it, and they will come. After twelve months, I could configure a KPI for leads, the conversion rate of leads to sales, the total number of new members we needed monthly, and the rate of monthly terminations. Each one of these KPIs can provide you a simple measure of where you will need to concentrate your efforts.

As I discussed earlier, you should have multiple sources for lead generation. Once these leads enter your funnel, track the efficiency of your conversion rate to a paying member. It's a volume game. Understand the 1,000 raving fans theory, from Kevin Kelley, and you'll remember you will not be a service for everyone. On the other side of the spectrum, if you observe a sales closing rate of less than 30%, you may want to re-evaluate your sales process. I'll later discuss this in more depth.

People will come and go. This is where understanding trends in the restaurant business can help you understand a concept of human behavior. Have you ever found a restaurant that you thoroughly enjoyed? Bloom intelligence, a company that tracks restaurant benchmarks, cites in its 2019 report[1] that if you visit a restaurant twice a month, it's considered favorable. Let's assume you dine at one of your favorite restaurants three to four times a month. After two years, you grew tired of the menu. You never had a poor meal in the place and their service is good. You are purely in the mood for something different. The longer you are open as a training facility, the higher the probability that you will experience this.

Attrition, or churn, is going to happen. What's important to realize is that it's going to happen, and you shouldn't make a person feel bad for leaving. If treated respectfully, people sometimes come back. People get divorced, have babies, and lose jobs. Life happens, and when these occurrences happen, you want to position yourself on the positive side. In Las Vegas, where I currently live, there is a local steakhouse my family and I frequent. The manager has been there for over fifteen years. He once shared that he sees a dip in covers every time a new restaurant opens in his proximity. He said years ago it bothered him, but he knows his regulars eventually come back. If the total number of new members exceeds the total amount of terminations, you will remain positive in growth.

The more data you collect on your business, the better you will be at predicting outcomes. Another important number you should track are cancellations of training sessions. Tracking the rate of monthly cancellations and aligning it with monitored terminations can provide insight into a trend you can minimize. Life happens, and within the parameters of people overbooked and overworked, cancellations of workouts are part of the territory. What you should monitor is if someone's monthly cancellations are increasing. That may be a sign of someone weaning in enthusiasm and in need of encouragement. Under the guidance of the best training program and coaching available, results will encounter plateaus. Training results are not linear. Having a system in place that notifies you of when a person exceeds a specific number of cancellations can be the difference between someone staying at your place or looking for the new shiny toy.

It's proven that it's easier and will cost you less to maintain a current member compared to what it cost, to get a new one through the door. A few simple and effective tactics we implement are restaurant gift cards mailed for birthdays, promotion of member-only contests, and member-only music playlists played on special occasions. Retention tactics frequently get overlooked instead of new member marketing. This is a time to get creative. Let your members feel like they are a part of something special. At J&D Fitness Personal Training, we have tracked the monthly retention rate from the day we opened our doors. I never allowed that number to drop below 85%. We will sacrifice marketing budget dollars for money spent on retention. This approach allowed us to sustain steady growth. It was our strong retention that played a huge role during the COVID-19 Pandemic. The retention formula we use is:

(MC – NM)/OMC)) x 100

MC = number of members at end of month

NM = number of new members gained during the period

OMC = number of members at the opening of the month

If during the start of the cycle you have 100 members, and factor in three terminations with nine new members, then you have 106 members at the end of the month. Using these numbers, your equation would look like this:

(106–9)/100 x 100 = 97% Retention rate

Greeting people when they enter your facility and offering a sweaty high five at the conclusion of a workout costs nothing and will pay dividends toward a high member retention rate.

The lifetime expectancy is a good metric to watch. This KPI can show you when members reach a goal and become restless, looking for a new challenge. Goal setting needs to be addressed beyond the initial consultation. Create a running, powerlifting, or obstacle course team within your studio. This is a way to create a new target.

Knowing how long an average member maintains an active membership in your facility provides you with insight into how much you can afford to spend to keep them.

MANAGING CASH FLOW

Not all debt is the same. There is a difference between good and bad debt. The determining factors are the payback terms (i.e., interest rates, length of the payback, stipulations etc.). High interest rate loans with short backpack terms have ended many businesses. This is one of the ways your accountant can provide value by discussing the terms of any loan under consideration. The interest may exceed your expected growth rate. You should strive to get initial loans for startup costs and expenses with conservative payback terms. Therefore, former or current training clients, family members, and friends are preferred resources. Using conservative estimates, eighteen months is a good benchmark to work toward being cash flow positive. That means after paying all monthly base expenses (including payroll), you have money left over. The faster you can achieve this, the better. Capital reserves will dictate the length of your financial runway. It's safe and a good idea to borrow more than you think you'll need. Unexpected expenses will occur. Downturns in the economy will happen. Who could have predicted two airplanes crashing into the World Trade Center, the financial crisis of 2008, or the pandemic of 2020?

A tactic I used that allowed me to become cash flow positive within my first year was to sublet prior to opening. I did some investigating and located a dance studio that was struggling financially. This was made evident due to their low traffic of customers during peak hours. I noticed that they only offered dance lessons in the evenings. I offered to pay a quarter of their monthly lease if they allowed me to come in and use their facility during the day. The beauty of functional training is that the equipment is very mobile. I had an architect who worked at the Coliseum theater in Caesars Palace on the Las Vegas Strip, construct a rig that allowed me to lower suspension trainers from the ceiling. When not in use, I pulled them up using a cable in a closet, like a curtain in a theater. I stored mats, foam rollers, kettlebells, and sandbags in a storage closet. In five minutes, I could transform the dance floor into a semi-private training studio.

Set up from my initial training studio subletting from a ballroom dancing studio

I used this setup to sell semi-private training memberships. I did this for one year. This is like when a big-box gym operates pre-sell promotions from a trailer on the construction site of the soon to open facility. Using this meager setup, I could get members. Not a large number, but it served two purposes.

Upon opening my studio, I had members to train from day one. It's easier to sell memberships to a gym that has people on the floor. Perception can become reality. It's not attractive to prospective members to join an empty studio. This provided me with a jump-start toward achieving cash flow positive status. I have observed many boutique gyms fail because they wait to sell until they open. Once you open the clock is ticking. The next benefit to subletting prior to opening was that I could beta-test how I would operate my training sessions. Understanding what worked and didn't work helped my decision-making when I started looking for a lease. I knew exactly the minimum space I needed to operate.

The custom rig that was fabricated to elevate the suspension trainers when the facility operated as ballroom dancing studio

Once you get past the first hurdle of earning cash flow positive status, you can work toward profitability and having a health EBITA. Earnings, before interest, taxes, and amortization (EBITA), is a measure of company profitability used by investors. Investopedia.com considers it a valuation used for comparison of one company to another in the same line of business. Sometimes, it can provide a more accurate view of the company's actual performance. This number extrapolates the profitability of a business after they pay all expenses. Gross revenue should not impress you, but the net income should. This is where some fall victim to making poor financial decisions.

PARADIGM 15

Embrace the process of learning how to decipher and understand financials. It is a skill and must be learned to be an effective operator.

PRICE SETTING

Most small gyms postpone pricing decisions until after they determine how they'll deliver the workout and the layout of the facility. They walk into their business hoping they can make money rather than know their business model will at the outset. Pricing guru and author of *Monetizing Innovation*, Madhavan Ramanujam, has made a career explaining that without a price, you literally don't have a product. He has a theory that you need to establish a price before the product. He's taken the popular term "product market fit" and expanded it to "product market price." I was lucky and had good business timing when I had to address this issue. In 2014, when I sold semi-private training, I wasn't the first. The market had proven that there was a demand. That's where I was lucky. The shift was toward selling large group or team training. This had grown from the popular outdoor boot-camp model that had existed previously. This also timed with the emergence and popularity of CrossFit and those type of gyms. The large group training model had groups of ten to twenty-five participants, sometimes larger. Semi-private training was in the minority, and that's where I had timing. I wish I could say I knew it would eventually shift toward semi-private, but it was more my personal bias and experience as a coach that drove me in that direction.

After accruing thirty years of training, I had learned the nuances of functional training, of how to coach suspension training, use kettlebells properly, and maximize the benefits of sandbags. I also learned how to communicate and coach using simple terms. I learned to identify the different ways people learned. Using these skills, I found it very challenging to coach over six people at once. During my stint at the ball room studio, I did briefly test coaching eight people at once. I determined I could do it, but it wasn't scalable. The skillset of the coach affected the user experience. There are large group training facilities that are operated well and run successfully. Semi-private training was my preference.

When it came time to establish a price, I noted that in a group of six people; I spent approximately a third of my time coaching a person directly, compared to when I worked with them solely. I took the fee I was charging for private coaching and divided it by a third. That may sound obvious, but many of the franchises that were offering large group training were charging half of what I was offering. It took courage on my behalf to set that price and stick to it. I was higher than my competitors, but from my perspective, I was offering a unique product. Using a restaurant analogy, I knew I didn't want to be a fast and casual type of place such as an Applebee's or Chili's. I wanted to be considered more a place that had white tablecloths and a nice wine list. Patrons enter a place such as that with different expectations. Mike Maples Jr., from the venture capital firm Floodgate, has stated, "Pricing is not a math problem, it's a psychology problem." I couldn't agree more. In semi-private training, you can come close to duplicating the touch and feel of private training. Committing to a lower price point, the consumer perceives it at good value.

Another key metric that I tracked was the average visits per month of each member. What I quickly saw was that people were privy to come in three to four times per week when exposed to semi-private training, compared to the twice per week standard of private training. This quickly translated to more training time, which produced better results. There is a science to pricing, it's not an art. When done correctly, your product can gain traction quickly. Using this price structure, I could charge a third of the price per visit, with the benefit of collecting half the revenue of private training monthly. This was because of the increased visitations per month.

Post 2010, many private training gyms shifted toward large group or semi-private training. This was partly because of their ability to charge a monthly membership and the ability to better scale the business. I disagreed with the many that discontinued private training. Upon opening the studio, I segmented my business by offering both private and semi-private training. Business segmentation is dividing your target audience into different sub-groups. The determining factors for us were training goals and any physical limitations. We could schedule our semi-private training sessions during peak hours and supplement that revenue with private training, which was scheduled throughout the day.

The global pandemic of 2020 from COVID-19 forced us to close. Upon re-opening, we quickly pivoted to promoting private training as an option to our members who were fearful to return to a group training environment. This quick change allowed us to respect the anxiety and fears caused by COVID-19 while maintaining our operation. We had enough coaches to accommodate. Some economists have written about how the pandemic accelerated some trends that were bound to happen eventually (working remotely, food delivery services, the usage of Zoom). It's my observation that with the improvements in quality coaching, that private training was due to make a resurgence in the upcoming years.

CAPITAL REINVESTMENT

It took me a few years to get a strategy and system for how much would be required annually for reinvestment. Under this category was money required for repair and maintenance, staff development, and new equipment purchases. Each one of these is vital for the longevity of your business. I understood the value, but I initially struggled with predicting costs. After a few years, I could track how much I was spending on each and then added that as a monthly expense to my BOE. After your initial build-out and purchase of new equipment, create a maintenance and repair log (MRL) to track any additional equipment, purchases, or repairs. You can then review annually and create a monthly allotment and budget for these expenses.

My experience in the industry taught me that new training modalities are always coming to the market. You need to stay abreast of new trends. I frequently observed how some gyms would become quickly dated by the workouts and the type of training they offered. I attended the International Health and Racquet Sport Club (IHRSA) trade show for the first time in 2005, in Las Vegas. One benefit of living in Las Vegas is that many conventions and conferences make Las Vegas a destination every couple of years. Providing an abundance of hotel rooms, ample conference space, and nightly entertainment has made Las Vegas a popular choice for trade shows and conventions. I attended IHRSA to get a perspective on upcoming trends. They often introduced new products in their beta-test format at this show. It was in 2015 that I observed less floor space designated for selectorized machines and an increase in displays of functional training equipment. Walking the trade show floor, IHRSA was a key contributor in helping me with the layout of what would eventually become the studio. Introduction of new equipment is a way to keep things fresh, but cost can become a factor. Establish an annual budget and make monthly contributions in preparation.

Once you purchase equipment, remember that it breaks. How many times have you observed a row of treadmills in a big-box gym, only to realize that half of them are broken? This does not exempt boutique gyms and studios from this frequent, and sometimes costly, expense. The number will increase in your first couple of years as your membership base and facility throughput increases. As a service business, you need to manage the capacity and flow of people into your facility daily. The amusement park industry has done a great job of this by creating and monitoring metrics related to this. Once you are operating at 60% capacity, the annual amount spent in your MRL should flatten out. Part of the decision-making process in equipment purchases should be the reliability warranty of the equipment. It was during this juncture that I chose Perform Better as a reliable vendor for equipment purchases. They are a leader in functional equipment, have excellent customer service, and stand by their products with good warranties.

Early in my training career, I made the decision that the best investment I could make in my career was my education. Certifications, continued education, and seminars became part of the norm for me. I observed how my income interconnected to my education. I don't equate education as credentials. You should choose competence over credentials. The more I learned, the better coach I became, the more results I could influence, and the more I could command for my services. This approach didn't stop once I opened my studio. I'll later discuss the importance and necessity of staff development. Understand that you need to establish a budget for staff development and education. After a couple of years of operations, I created an annual calendar of studio sponsored education. This included not only the cost of certifications, conferences, and training summits but also lodging. Contribute to this monthly to avoid a large disruption to your monthly cash flow.

PARADIGM 16

A business is a living organism. If you stop feeding it, in the form of reinvestment,
it will slowly wither away and die.

CHAPTER 6

OPERATIONS- THE REALITY IS MESSY AND COMPLEX

IN 2011, I listened to the physical therapist and strength coach, Gray Cook, lecture at a Training Summit about the Functional Movement Screen (FMS). The FMS is an assessment screen that Cook and cofounder, Lee Burton, developed in 1997. I was familiar with the screen and was learning how to use it during my training practice. In his talk, Cook discussed how the beauty within the FMS was the ease of application and the lack of needing a licensed physical therapist to administer. They had taken a complicated problem and created a simple process using a system. Soon after, I read *The Checklist Manifesto*, by Atul Gawande. This book shares multiple stories about how the use of a checklist can reduce human error in the completion of multi-step tasks in complex professions. Gawande accounts the high total of error because of the void of a system. A typical challenge in a service business is to deliver the service consistently. A typical approach taken is to gain more training and experience, with the goal of reaching a level of mastery in the skill. The problem with that approach is that you are striving to become an expert.

As an expert, you come across two distinct problems. The first problem is human memory and attention. This is especially common in the mundane tasks. As a trainer, I can remember how my ability to count and keep track of repetitions became worse as I became a better coach. It was a common joke among my clients about how poorly I kept count. My focus had shifted toward watching their movement patterns, alignment, and their breath patterns. My attention had shifted. I soon found out that this was a common predicament within the trainer spectrum. Once I opened the studio and we shifted more toward timed intervals using a timer, those complaints disappeared. Engineers call distractions and a mistake riddled memory the all-or-none processes.

The second problem is that you can lull yourself to sleep as you perform the task and then commit missteps. This is truly clear in complex tasks, where every step may not be as important as the other. A common example of this in the fitness world is when a coach can't remember which leg you just performed a drill with. I'll use the lunge to explain. The client finishes the set and then asks, "Which leg did I just do?" The coach (more focused on knee alignment, force production, and trunk position) responds with, "I don't know." This is a simple example of how an error can happen not because of incompetency, but the lack of a list where the coach could simply follow. Prioritization and starting with the weaker leg first can fix that. The client would always finish on the stronger leg.

Early on (prior to 2000) in the training, strength, and conditioning profession, these problems didn't occur in volume. The coaching prowess was minimal, which enabled the trainer to focus on counting and cheering. I can remember in my early days of coaching at Bally's Health in Fitness in the '90s referring to these trainers as "clipboard cowboys." They walked around with a clipboard. On that clipboard was a breakdown of the weight the members used as they traveled through each machine in their circuit or what they had named the thirty-minute workout. Once they had the person on the machine with the proper height and seat adjustments, all they had to do was count. You could hear echoes of "Eight, nine, you got it, you got it, ten," throughout the gym floors in the '90s. That changed in the 2000s. Coaches became smarter because of the availability and affordability of education. Organizations and equipment manufacturers realized that there was money to be made in teaching a growing profession. As the quality of coaching improved, the quality of counting worsened.

What the industry understood is that coaching and personal training is complicated, as stated by two professors who study the science of complexity- Brenda Zimmerman of York University and Sholom Glouberman of the University of Toronto.

"Complicated problems are ones like sending a rocket to the moon. They can sometimes be broken down into a series of simple problems. But there is no straightforward recipe. Success frequently requires multiple people, often multiple teams, and specialized expertise."[1]

It's common among veteran coaches to state the old classic mantra of, the more I know, the more I realize what I didn't know. As we grew to understand things, such as how the amount of load affected the body, exercise intensity, and the quality of movement, the need for having a checklist grew in importance. You should document your operations and the format of how you present your workout from the moment your patrons enter to their exit.

The aim of operations is to create a plan of action. When problems occur, we should note it with a course of action on how to handle the situation. Like the operating system within a computer, you want to follow a program. If a bug happens, create the fix and update. As in writing software for a new program, the biggest challenge is the initial coding of the program. Over time, the program, or operation's plan, will get better by the corrections and adjustments made to handle problems. You should welcome scrutiny and debate on the best practice to the plan of action. This process is the creation of your system. It's the series of systems that become the lifeblood of running your business.

PARADIGM 17

Every action that is expected to be consistently duplicated within the confines of your business should be documented and critiqued and continually improved. This allows each action to be quantified as an action plan or system. These systems create the skeleton of your business operation.

Upon opening my studio in 2015, I had attained twenty-three years of education and experience in personal training. Many of the pioneers in the fitness, strength, and conditioning industry influenced me. It was easy for me to lean upon my experience every time I worked with someone to create an individual program. As a past, free-lance personal trainer, my immediate course of action was to personalize everything as much as possible on the fly. After hiring a team of coaches, who in most likelihood will not possess the amount of experience as me, showed how that approach wasn't scalable. The lack of a plan on how to deliver your service doesn't provide you with the confidence to predict a positive outcome for your patron. I soon after created a standard operating system that would deliver our training service to each of our members. We frequently tested, challenged, and updated until we reached a point when we could duplicate it over and over, with the same outcome.

To understand the value of having an operating system, you

can look at the popularity of franchises in the last twenty years. Purchasing a franchise allows an owner to bypass building the business systems and instead use a system that has already proven to be successful. That's a smart step. The only foreseeable obstacle I see with that plan may be the barrier to entry. Franchises have an initial franchise fee, plus marketing fees and royalties. The US Small Business Administration reports that these fees "Can range from $20,000-$50,000, unless you're considering purchasing a Master Franchise. (Master franchises involve purchasing a large geographical area and selling franchises in that area.) The franchise fee for a Master Franchise can run $100,000 or more."[2] This doesn't include the initial cost of starting the business. The relationship within franchises can become strained. It's not uncommon for franchisees to disagree with how the brand is being marketed. Lawsuits between both parties, franchisor and franchisee, are common because one side believes the other is not fulfilling their commitment under the terms of their agreement.

A benefit of starting as a free-lance personal trainer and then learning how to be an operator is that you should have the skill set of coaching. The trap of some coaches and trainers is that they spend a large majority of their time reviewing workouts and programs and never switching gears to focus on the delivery of the workout. Operations in a boutique gym is a documented protocol of how you will deliver services once a person enters your facility. A system doesn't depend on inspiration or on being in a good mood. An operating system is agnostic to the administration of the system. An operating system is the blueprint for running the day-to-day tasks within your business.

THE FIRST IMPRESSION

When you walk into a building, and someone greets you, how do you feel? If they make eye contact, form a smile, and say hello, it probably leaves a positive feeling. Amy Cuddy, a social psychologist from Harvard Business school, explains that when we meet someone for the first time, we're forming two impressions. The initial impression is trying to determine how trustworthy and warm is this person. The second impression is trying to answer the question, "What are this person's intentions toward me?" We're also asking ourselves, "How strong and competent is this person?" Research has proven that these two traits account for 80% to 90%of an overall first impression and that holds true across cultures.[3] Having a system on how you will greet every person who enters your gym is a good starting point.

We all remember watching the popular 80s sitcom, Cheers, and how everyone greeted Norm every time he entered. Large corporations such as Walmart and Starbucks have invested substantially in greeting their patrons as they enter. In a boutique gym, you will have a smaller membership base compared to a larger big-box gym. This environment enables you the ability to greet your members by name. Danny Meyer, CEO of Union Square Hospitality Group and founder of Shake Shack, wrote in his book, *Setting the Table*, about the value of making your customer feel special. As a leader in hospitality, he embraced technology as a useful tool. In his restaurants, it was common for them to document birthdays, special occasions, and favorite tables in a database. If you dine in one of his eateries, you can expect to be greeted by a host with a reference to the last time you were in. "Virtually nothing else is as important as how one is made to feel in any business transaction."[4]

Once you greet your patron, they should know where they can put their belongings and where they can change, if needed. If you have a check-in system, this is an appropriate time to explain that format. The availability of workout towels is a value-added convenience and helps maintain a level of cleanliness within the studio. If the facility offers this service, communicate that to the new member. They should summarize retail items, such as bottled water, with an explanation of how to purchase. Designate an area where a person goes at the start of the workout. A key step is to eliminate assumptions on behalf of your member.

An obvious mistake frequently made in training gyms is assuming that a person will know what to do. Consider that there is a high probability that this is the first time a person has been in a gym. You know for sure that they have never been in your facility. The next thing to note is that the new member's anxiety is going to be elevated. The gym industry has done their share between advertisements and social media of getting out the message that pain and discomfort are part of exercise. People are expecting discomfort and looking silly. You should make every attempt to dispel this myth.

Humans are wired to avoid pain and failure. No one wants to feel ignorant or incompetent attempting things they cannot do. I call this walking into a dark room syndrome. If you have ever walked into a completely dark room, one of your instincts will be to put your hands out in front of you. Having your visual sense taken away, you immediately put your hands out in front to avoid walking into anything. People coming into a training studio commonly experience similar fear. It's the fear of the unknown. An effective way to combat this is to provide insight and tell them what to expect.

An example of dialogue you may use is:

Coach: Hi Jon, welcome to the studio. I'm glad you made it today. You can put your keys and bag in our cubbies over here. Do you have water?

Jon: Yes.

Coach: Good. If you run out, we have drinking fountains or bottled water, you can purchase. As your coach for today's session, it's my responsibility to check you in. The restrooms are in the back of the studio if you need to use the bathroom. The studio provides a workout towel which you can use today. Please put it in the basket by the door on your way out. Let's go over to the warm-up area and I can explain what you can expect in today's workout. Please, feel free to ask me any questions you may have.

An explanation of what to expect, accompanied by a smile, can go a long way in making a person feel welcomed. You should have a designation on who performs this with a prepared script. You can perform it individually or in a group. Once someone enters your facility, strive to provide more than just a workout, but an experience. It should be your objective to orchestrate this occurrence so that it is positive.

PARADIGM 18

Script out the perfect experience in your gym. Then reverse engineer the process by listing each step. That process becomes a cog in your system. Don't leave making people feel good as an outcome of luck. You can systematize good hospitality.

THE WORKOUT

Workouts will vary based on the training modality. The focus of this book is not on training or program design, but a blueprint for establishing a delivery system for your workout. Regardless of what equipment you use, training philosophy, or chosen modality, you should have a documented program. This program should be concise and documented so that fellow coaches can duplicate the execution of the workout. The coaches who will administer the training session should understand all languages and terms used.

Inform your coaches and staff of expectations and outcomes of the people you expect them to work with. Based upon the model of your workout, there may be a set of exercise standards with regressions and progressions. Outline in an operation manual what those are. The goal within an operational setting should be to focus on the execution of a well thought out plan with minimal energy spent on creation. Take into consideration all assessments and screens. The job of the coach should be to navigate the member through the session. All workouts will have a beginning, a middle, and a conclusion. These sections should be clear and without confusion for the coach to follow.

Upon completion of the workout, there should be a formal closing of the session signaling completion to the member. The closing should include a form of positive praise for completing the session. Common industry examples are a high five or fist pump. Plan a professional form of praise for your team to use. Feedback and praise are staples, and your team should perform at the close of every training session. Like writing a business letter which has a greeting, body, and friendly close, your workout should have a similar format.

WHY USE A SCRIPT

In the past, a common approach taken by some boutique studio operators on delivering workouts was to focus on training the coach. Once the coach achieved a level of competency, they then progressed to work with the members. That was the extent of their operational system to deliver a workout or training session. You should train your staff, and I'll discuss this in employee development, but it should be on the delivery of your system. You should have a pre-arranged workout, thus leaving the coach as the one to deliver the product. In this scenario, the product is the workout. Standards should be in place that allow the coach to either regress or progress the workout. You need to establish a language within your studio that clearly communicates to the coach when and what those regressions or progressions can be. This can be achieved by teaching concepts in lieu of exercises only. Your goal is to minimize the total amount of gray area that exists within the training session. Here's an example of how we achieve this:

In today's training session, we have an overhead press using a kettlebell. The person has to have a score of two or better from their assessment (Functional Movement Screen) to perform the exercise. If they don't, they regress to a thoracic spine mobility drill, such as a thoracic spine rotation, using the suspension trainer. The progression for the movement is a bottom's up isometric hold performed with the kettlebell, which requires additional shoulder stability and grip strength, compared to the traditional overhead version.

You should prepare everything about the workout in advance. Technology has helped in this area. There are apps available which can list the workouts, including all regressions or progressions. The key is to eliminate the step of program design for the coach. Program design is a separate designation.

Good coaching is not robotic. Coaches can stamp their individual personality into every training session by the use of humor and energy. That is where management can empower their team by allowing them to inject their individualism. A coach may interpret the control of what they perform in a workout as an insult to their skill level. As the art of training has grown in complexity, we can no longer leave it to a lone hero's expertise. You must communicate as a team. This is where templates and lists are very effective. Program design is preordained. The coach's role now shifts to good communication and passion. That is a vital part of the equation.

During the creation process of your workout, you need to create a template. This template will allow you to scale your workouts and consistently duplicate. An efficient approach is to look at your workouts like an auto assembly line from the Industrial Revolution. Each stop along the line allows the worker to add or assemble their cog into the finished product. This approach is not to belittle the need of your members. You may offer different workouts with different outcome goals. The comparison between your gym and an auto manufacturer is like comparing workouts with different outcome goals (fat loss, strength improvement, and enhance mobility) to a plant that produces different automobile models. What you want to focus on is the delivery of the workout.

Review and audit workouts for consistency and quality. Establish a role of quality control and assign it to a team member who will routinely check that the workouts are being properly executed. Scrutinize training sessions for efficacy. Did it deliver? The time required for this task will rest solely upon the volume of training sessions. Training programs are structured from hypothesizes, philosophies, and principals. Laws are derived from principles. Principles represent the accepted moral and/or ethical standards of any group or society; they do not carry the force of law, but they do underpin the processes by which laws acceptable to the group or society are debated, formulated, and approved. That means we can challenge principals and philosophies. Scientific laws do not change, nor are they created, but they are discovered.

When learning a language, a common first step is to memorize some vocabulary. After building a base of words, you can group them in phrases. The next progression is to put sentences together. It's important to understand the culture of the language. This provides context and, in certain situations, will allow a better understanding. You may have heard the saying, "It's all Greek to me." This is an idiom in English referring to an expression that it is hard to understand for the speaker[5]. In order to communicate with someone else, you must speak the same language. This concept is why you must create a resource for your coaches that lists every exercise and movement they will be responsible to administer.

Early in training centric gyms and studios, the differentiator between an average and above average coach was their depth of knowledge of exercises. I would go a step further than that and say they may not have understood the concept behind the exercise but possessed a good recall of the exercises. In the internet's era, with the addition of social media, there should no longer exist a shortage of exercises to draw from. No one can out-think the internet. Each gym should have a menu of exercises they use that apply to their philosophy of training. An example of this is if you use kettlebells at your facility and program squats into the training programs of your members, compile a list of all squat variations using the kettlebell. A sequence of all exercises used at your facility becomes the common language spoken by your coaches and trainers.

Maintaining the business objective to provide a consistent experience for your consumer is a step that should be evident. Like a restaurant, part of cooking the same dish by multiple cooks is to use the same ingredients. The preparation of the dish may have a couple of differences, as a coach may use different cues, but you want to minimize those variations.

The equipment manufacturers made this step easier as many of them created courses and education on how to use their equipment. This included safety steps, acronyms, and a vocabulary for the exercises. You have the option to adopt their protocol (if it aligns with your system) or create your own. This goes back to understanding your consumer.

In 2012, I became certified as a coach by the Russian Kettlebell Challenge (RKC) to instruct the use of kettlebells. In this certification, I was taught and tested on my proficiency on the "big six" movements using kettlebells. This included the:

- Clean
- Swing
- Snatch
- Turkish get-up
- Squat
- Overhead press

In each of the above listed movements, there are specific protocols that deem the exercise safe for the person to attempt the drill. In this system, you teach using a specific progression. Pavel Tsatsouline created the program for Dragon Door publications, to standardize how kettlebells are taught and coached. Pavel receives much of the credit as the one who introduced kettlebells to the United States. Standardizing a common vernacular is a pillar in solid operations.

You can categorize by movement patterns or equipment, but there needs to be a formal listing of all exercises used. Online videos, tutorials, and instructor apps can make this process easier. This breakdown of exercises and movements creates a standard of practices for the facility.

YOUR OPERATIONS MANUAL

The way you greet your members, the format of your training session, and an encyclopedia of exercises used in your facility are a few of the things you should have in your operations manual. The manual should have everything required to run your gym. I'm surprised by the minimal time owners spend refining this process. If you can't put it in writing, it doesn't exist. This also creates a simple way for your team to find the answer to questions they may have. Consider your operation's manual as the Google search on how to run your gym. The creation of a manual will require time. It should document processes and protocols for running your facility. These are steps that can take up to three years to refine as accepted practice. The drafting of the manual should not be rushed. It should act as a reference for all staff. It will eliminate some of the mundane questions from staff and reduce the frequency of interruptions. As you grow, it should streamline the development of staff.

The manual should include (but not limited to):

- Position requirements, job tasks, and responsibilities
- Required work attire
- Mission statement
- Vision statement
- Core values
- Code of conduct
- Training philosophy
- Program format
- Warm-ups, exercises, and movement preparatory drills
- How to request time off
- How to open and close facility
- First aid and safety protocols
- Emergency evacuation
- Required reading
- A place to record passwords and usernames for company software log-ins

The communication between you and your team is precious. You may desire for your staff to hang onto your every word, but things get lost or missed in the current noisy environment. Organizing your expectations and the value system of your facility in one place can help keep everyone on the same page. Don't fall into the trap of writing lengthy mission statements that only look good on paper and create a minimal effect on staff behavior. The vision statement of J & D Fitness Group is:

"To create an experience where empowered coaches can guide and encourage others to improve."

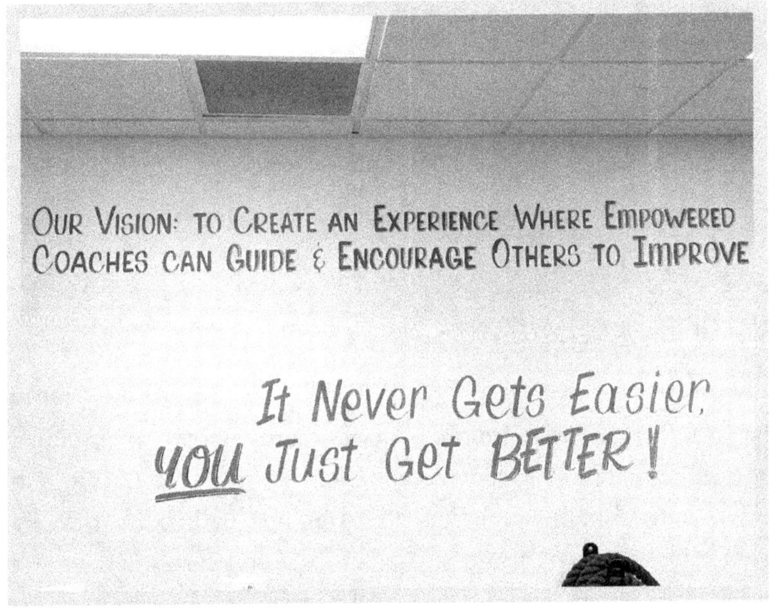

Our vision statement is on a studio wall as a daily reminder of what we strive to accomplish.

After we were open for three years, the entire staff sat down together and developed our core values as a team. That exercise was valuable and allowed me to draw upon it when we drifted away from those values.

List all exercises with the regressions and progressions within your manual. Keep these organized and easy to reference. New hires will find this valuable in the beginning. It also reinforces the expectations of what you expect your coaches to know and understand. This will change overtime, but digital format makes updates and edits simple. As your business matures, so will your manual. You should review it periodically, editing and updating it as you see appropriate.

PARADIGM 19

Everything required to run and operate your studio should be documented in an operation's manual.
If it's not documented, it doesn't exist.

VALUE OF A CLEAN GYM

Cleanliness within the gym world has improved. Dirty bathrooms, unkept training floors, and poorly maintained equipment are no longer acceptable. The new boutique gym offers natural lighting, designed entries, and bathrooms that are well kept. Once upon a time, you could put off cleaning to once a week. Those days are over. In a well-run facility, you should have a cleaning checklist that is used daily. Hire a cleaning company. Personal trainers and coaches want to coach, not clean. Salespeople should focus on the needs of the people interested in joining your gym. If you expect your sales team and coaches to mop floors and clean bathrooms, you should include it in their description during the hiring process. Coaches should maintain an uncluttered working area by returning and racking equipment when not in use. In the micro-gym (gyms less than 10,000 square feet), floor space is a commodity. Use storage racks and keep things off the floor. Storage racks have improved in design and are no longer eyesores.

The training gym is now competing with workouts available at home. The level of cleanliness should not be a factor in deciding which option is a better fit for the consumer. Consumers expect gyms to be clean in the current landscape of fitness offerings. Gyms that were poorly maintained and dirty struggled during the global pandemic. In a reactive stance, some gyms pulled up flooring and painted interior walls to disguise their lack of a satisfactory cleaning protocol. A clean gym is a benefit and can attract new members. As an operator, walk your floor frequently and inspect for cleanliness. A clean facility should be a standard protocol, not an upgrade of service.

Once you get past the phase of wishing people will use your services and you have a steady flow of customers, you need to keep equipment maintained. Poorly maintained equipment is not only a poor look professionally, it's a liability. If your studio is successful, equipment is going to break. You should have a budget and should be able to predict the cost of replacing equipment. Coaches and trainers will have a role in this responsibility. Each time they use a piece of equipment, they should know it's wear. If they find a piece of equipment that is suspect of breaking soon, they should immediately bring it to the attention of management. Running a gym in Las Vegas, I observed how the dry climate can speed up the wear on bands and tubing. No one enjoys using a stability ball that bursts or a band that abruptly snaps. Don't expect luck to help you see a piece of equipment that is on the verge of breaking. Create a safety checklist that is used periodically to inspect all equipment.

HOW TO KEEP THEM AFTER YOU GET THEM

Member and client retention are not as challenging as you may think. It requires you to follow through on the promises you made before they gave you money. The trap some coaches and trainers fall into is to relax on their laurels once they receive that month's payment. That's the beginning. Now the real work starts. The moment you get someone to commit, the partnership between coach and participant has started. Your goal is to over deliver on the promises you initially made.

Create a welcome postcard that is sent out once they join. This serves multiple purposes. It can be a marketing tool, as people may put it on a fridge or cork board in their home. This serves as a conversation piece. People are prone to share stories with family and friends about making positive decisions. Committing to exercise three days a week with a trainer is a badge of honor. A card thanking them for their patronage is a simple visual tool that can act as a business card for your business, but also a pat on the back, making a step in a positive direction. A new member is more likely to post a picture of the welcome postcard they received from their new gym on social media, then a post about sleeping in on their first workout.

Postcards acknowledging joining the gym, first workouts, birthdays, and their anniversary of joining are simple ways to make people feel special. The cost is minimal, and the return can be substantial. One of the KPI's I closely monitor is our member retention rate. This number should improve over time. It's based upon providing what your people want. The more you get to know your members, the more you should be able to cater to their needs. It requires T&T, technology and time.

Surveys are very popular. Retailers fill the inbox of your email with surveys. They are popular because they are easy to distribute digitally, and they work. A survey sent from a boutique gym will carry more weight than a survey sent from a large retail chain because the person feels the survey from the gym is going to be seen. Surveys are valuable not for the applause and kudos on how things are perfect, rather the insight to when someone isn't happy. It allows you to correct a problem that may fester within your facility. To affirm this theory, you can use the success of Yelp. Yelp is a digital, democratic survey service. It allows a user to share their experience, whether good or bad. When creating your survey, minimize the number of questions (five or fewer), and make the answers multiple choice. Surveys in this format have proven to be completed. It helps if you can also reward the member with a gift or prize if they complete the survey.

Surveys also empower you to grow your studio. In the beginning, they forced you to guess. Until you have users to provide feedback, you are not sure if the outcome you desire will materialize. Questions about optimal training times when members like to come to your facility, which workouts they enjoy the most, and needs they don't feel are being addressed. Once you open, you can now answer these questions. The feedback you receive from surveys is a valuable tool. We have referenced data as the oil of this generation. The acquisition and collection of data has been the source of substantial fortunes in technology companies. Data is not only valuable in the technology sector. User data is valuable in all C to B businesses.

Birthdays are a good way to celebrate your members. Besides sending a card in the mail, we include a gift card to a local restaurant. It's a token of appreciation. This tactic comes with a cost. The card, postage, and gift card have hard costs associated. Another tactic we use is to offer our members to supply us with a music playlist that we play during their workout on their birthday. This costs nothing and creates immense value toward member experience. We created guidelines. Songs can't have profanity. They must email the playlist to our operation's manager a week before. It's limited to fourteen songs. Outside of the time needed to load the playlist within our music provider, the investment is minimal and the return substantial.

Country clubs have mastered the art of retention for years. They foster a community of members that feel like the club is theirs. The cost to join these clubs of exclusivity creates that vibe. They do not provide everyone access. A boutique studio can have a similar environment. Because the facility is not large, you can create a sense of limited accessibility. Having a capacity for only two hundred people should be an asset, not a liability.

Hosting member-only events is a unique and valuable retention tool. It's unique because you can cater to what your people like. At our studio, I created a J & D Fitness Olympics. The events would vary from year to year, but the premise was to have multiple fitness events where each member can compile points. I awarded winners crystal trophies and the title of a winner for the year. It is a big draw, and we get 30-40% of our members to take part. We have events such as timed bodyweight rows using a suspension trainer, weighted sled pushes for distance, and overhead presses with sandbags for reps. The premise is that if you train in our facility, you will excel in these activities. Along with re-enforcement of your training philosophy, you can build on your gym culture. To see a large example of this, look at the popularity of the CrossFit games.

The more mature your business becomes, the more you should shift dollars from the marketing budget toward revenue for member retention. You can spend this money more strategically and it is less than money spent on new member acquisition.

> ## PARADIGM 20
> The marketing and member retention budgets should be diametrically opposed. As your business matures and your member base grows you should be able to shift funds out of marketing and more toward member retention.

DON'T TAKE IT PERSONALLY

People are going to leave. Couples get divorced, people move, illnesses happen. The worst thing you can do is make someone feel bad that they can no longer be a member of your gym. Use that as an opportunity to thank them for their business and acknowledge you will always welcome them to return. Rude treatment to a member because they lost their job is unacceptable and shouldn't be tolerated. That is a guaranteed way to confirm that a person doesn't return once their circumstances change. We have a system of putting their email on a separate list and sending out emails periodically catered specifically to this group. Re-activations can happen. Include them as part of your sales funnel. Living in Las Vegas for the past nineteen years, I've experienced both boom and bust economies. After gaming and tourism, then mining (the Silver State), logistics and manufacturing are our largest industries.[6] We've had members move to other states during down times, only to return during economic upswings.

People leaving your studio or terminating their membership create a separate category you can market to. This group qualifies as ideal candidates for re-activation. If your facility caters to a general population demographic, this is ideal. If you offer sports performance programming, which can lead to seasonal training, this also qualifies. Over the long haul, you will have people step out of the fold only to return a year or two later. Re-activation clients can grow to become 3%-5% of your membership base and should not be ignored.

THE DIRTY WORD- SALES

If you plan on making money training people, you are going to have to create a sales process. Many of the experts will tell you that all sales are the same. "We're all selling something." I would agree partially with that statement. What my experience has showed to me over the years is that sales in personal training are unique. Sales in personal training require active listening and empathy on behalf of the salesperson and continual follow-through from the eventual member. Emotions may motivate someone to make the initial meeting, but buy-in will get them to come back. Sales are converting leads and prospects into members of your gym. Track your percentage of closing a viable lead into a member. Monitoring that percentage can notify you of when you need to focus on your sales process.

I applaud every person who enters our studio who is interested in hiring a trainer. It takes courage and a level of vulnerability to share with someone that you need help and will pay someone if they can help. The job of the salesperson is to find out and dig a little deeper under the surface to find out exactly what the person wants. As the story goes, the person walking into Home Depot to buy a shelf to hang isn't looking for a shelf, but rather they are looking to get rid of clutter.

Start your sales process by determining the problem. If the prospect shares what their problem is, without questioning, they have made your job easy. At that point, determine the solution and if it aligns with your services, sign them up. You will need to perform some digging in most cases. Engage with them. Ask probing questions. If you want to help the person, you'll need to know the ailment. Where do they want to go? They may not know. You may have to assist by defining and helping them to create goals. They may not know they have a problem, but feel they need to do something. The next step is to figure out if your process can fix the problem.

This is the big difference between general access gyms and training centric facilities. In a general access gym, the member can come in and use the facility. There is no structure for their workout. Many of the large big-box gyms thrive in this market because only 10-15% of their member base are active users. They focus the sales process in this business model on emotion and make it easy for the person to join, understanding that a large majority will never come in. The weakness of this model appeared in the early days of the global pandemic. Members of these gyms were quick to cancel their gym memberships and were slow to return.

In the training gym, you want your members to come in. It's a simple model. The more they come in and have access to structured coaching, the more benefit they get. These gyms typically experience a higher retention rate than general access facilities. People are less prone to discontinue services that are providing value.

As a certified trainer, I use strength and conditioning as my hammer to fix things. You're going to come across scenarios when someone needs a screwdriver and not a hammer to fix the problem. In those cases, refer them to the appropriate professional. An example is when guidance from a medical doctor or physical therapist is needed. Your first responsibility is to do no harm. Accept that you cannot fix every problem that comes through your doors. The true professional understands and accepts this.

If you deduce your services will benefit the prospect, then the next step is to explain your fee structure. Present it clearly and unapologetically. Sales in personal training may start out emotionally driven but should end rationally. That person woke up on that day and decided, "Today is the day." Good. They then took action and contacted you, even better. Now you take that bit of inspiration and explain to them it is going to be a process. Don't bog them down with all the details of every exercise. You are providing the GPS to get them to their end destination.

If you receive an inquiry through either email or a phone call, ask them to stop by your gym so you can explain your services. Most people calling around for prices never make it down to the gym. Don't give prices over the phone. You want someone to purchase your services for the value you provide, not because you are the cheapest person in town. If they aren't willing to spend twenty minutes talking with you at your gym about their goals, then they probably aren't willing to spend the time it's going to take to reach their aspirations. Training for strength, mobility, or performance all requires a commitment of time. Requesting someone to come in to discuss your services is setting the table for what lies ahead.

> ## PARADIGM 21
> Each step of the customer acquisition process should be documented, including the cost to gain the customer. Customer acquisition cost is a key KPI.

Coaches should coach, and salespeople should sell. I believe you keep them separate, but you can have someone perform both job responsibilities. Just be aware that they are two distinct skill sets. Many gyms will require coaches' prospect for their training clients. The problem with that is that many coaches get into the profession to coach and help people. They don't possess the skills in how to market or sell their services. You should have designated people who fit the role of a salesperson. That allows them to concentrate on converting leads generated from your marketing arm into members. Another option is to have a person who may perform both roles of a trainer and a salesperson in a hybrid model. Clearly define the position and pay structure. Understand that if you have a person committing part time to sales, that you are going to receive a part-time return on their sales efforts.

If you require coaches to prospect for their training clients, be forthcoming in the interview process and job description. Keeping that responsibility undisclosed in the hiring process is an unethical practice. That tactic is a key reason behind high turnover rates in coaches at many training gyms.

PART FOUR

CHAPTER 7

HIRING YOUR TEAM

YOU DON'T VALUE the importance of hiring good people until you bring on a staff. The first hurdle is making the choice to hire someone. Many people shy away from hiring people due to the responsibility of paying them that comes with it. Good month or awful month, people expect to get paid. Payroll will be one of your largest liabilities. This will add to the anxiety that you are learning on the job and will make tons of mistakes. For inspiration, look at top CEOs, such as Reed Hastings of Netflix, Steve Jobs of Apple, and Mark Zuckerberg of Facebook for examples of owners who learned on the job. I trust most successful CEOs will tell you they are light years in professional development beyond from when they started. A key realization is when you understand the traits and characteristics an employee must have to thrive in the position that for which you have hired them.

Each position and role should have a clear description of the skills needed for the employee. Avoid the obvious high energy and good character clichés. Peel the onion back and determine the mindset and personality traits needed for each role. In my business model, I would teach them everything about coaching. I prefer that they have minimal coaching experience. This allows you to work with a blank canvas and avoids them bringing bad past habits. In the documentary film, *Andre and his Olive Tree* on Netflix, featuring Taiwan's First Michelin-Starred Chef-Restaurateur, André Chiang, chef André shares that when he's hiring, he doesn't look for the chefs to have knife skills for chopping or slicing. "I don't care if they can't chop, I'll show them." He looks for people to have an ingrained work ethic and a commitment to getting better. We can say the same about hiring a coach. Look beyond their competency in teaching lifts and more toward their ability to complete a task and how quickly they can gain new skills.

It goes back to your core values. Allow that to guide you in the hiring process. As stated by Gino Wickman in *Traction: Get a Grip on Your Business*, "It's important to note that whatever your core values are, they don't make them good or bad. They just don't fit in your company culture."[1]

The life of a coach can translate into challenging hours. Hours of demand are early mornings and late evenings. When hiring, I look to see if that bothers people. Coaches must accept that schedule as a demand for the job. The ability to focus is another key part of being a coach. Through the coaching experience, you teach, engage, observe, and then continually provide feedback. A breakdown in focus will affect the desired outcome. Like the rocket heading to space constantly adjusting, a coach is always tweaking things.

One of the most valuable assets I appreciate in a new hire is their ability to learn quickly. I teach my coaches everything and expect upon starting out, they will have a minimal understanding of exercise. I expect them to have a high cognitive ability. The skill of learning and then later applying that skill to problem solve is a valuable trait of coaching. A classic example of this is when you teach the squat. At the training studio, we use a variety of different squats as a drill. For example:

- Bodyweight squat
- Suspension trainer assisted squat
- Split squat
- Kettlebell goblet squat
- Suspension trainer front squat
- Contralaterally loaded squat with sandbag

The coach, when assigning the exercise, is to meet the person at their skill level, take into consideration their movement competency, and select the appropriate exercise. The consistent question that needs to be addressed is "for what and for whom." What are you trying to achieve and who are you asking to perform the drill? That question helps you to narrow your options when choosing drills. A coach needs to draw from the exercise database within their mind and choose an option in a relatively brief timeframe.

How do you determine if someone is a quick learner? Years ago, I came across a brain teaser game by the company, Thinkfun. A friend brought the game to my attention as something I could play with my son, who at the time was ten. It's a STEM game encouraging children to develop logic and work through fun challenges. The goal is to build a brick wall using the five unique configured pieces. The game comes accompanied with playing cards that show you the shape of the wall on one side with a pictured diagram explanation on the other side. It's a game of problem solving and logic. As the owner of a boutique studio, I will teach the coach, but I need them to comprehend. I created a game I use with interviews. First, they see the shape of the wall they need to build. Next, I explain how the pieces fit. I give them a couple of minutes to study the card. I then flip the card over and ask them to create the wall in time. This drill has provided me with wonderful insight into the person sitting across from me during an interview. I once had a woman almost start crying when she couldn't figure out the puzzle. I did not hire her. This unorthodox step in an interview allows me to see how people react when things don't work out as expected. The goal is not to upset the candidate, but to observe how someone can learn in a low stress situation. It provides a larger picture of who the person is.

In the hiring process, you accept it takes a unique person to work for a non-established or young business. There is no guarantee that you will survive. You should be transparent with this reality. The interview process works both ways. They are determining whether you are someone they want to work for. Hiring comes with its challenges and is a skill. It can be time-consuming, but you should be relentless. Nothing will play a larger role in the success of your gym than the quality of your hiring. Take the time to get better at it.

PARADIGM 22

Create a detailed description of the ideal employee. Focus on personality traits as opposed to credentials when possible. Use these traits when recruiting and building your team.

One of the best tips I can provide regarding hiring is to learn from your mistakes. Reflect on those that become good hires and those that don't develop into ideal team members. A mistake I made early on was not clearly explaining what professional conduct is. One of my coaches had a tense verbal exchange with a member during a workout. He took it upon himself to text her later in the day, stating he didn't appreciate her comments and that we did not welcome her at the studio. The correct thing to do was to contact me and allow me to handle the situation. I could have used that opportunity to educate the coach on how to handle someone when you are entangled in a combative situation and praise him for coming to me. Instead, he was abusive and used inappropriate and derogatory language in a text message. The text was not the only problem in this situation; he didn't think his behavior was inappropriate. The member brought it to my attention immediately, and the coach was terminated. What I learned from that incident was that I need to communicate with all team members when it's appropriate to contact a member, and how they can speak to them. I outlined this in a code of conduct and after that incident have each new hire sign it after we review it together during their onboarding. Treat professionalism like coaching and assume nothing.

CHAPTER 8

SKILL AND WILL

ANDY GROVE, past chair and CEO of Intel, wrote in his book, *High Output Management*, "That all you can do to improve the output of an employee is to train and motivate." Operating and running Intel during some of its most productive years, Grove followed a mantra of consistently improving the skill level of his staff along with elevating their motivation. A past client of mine, Del Yocam, once COO of Apple, once shared with me that it was the training he received while employed at Ford (his prior employer) that helped him to be an effective manager during his years at Apple. I have trained several past and current CEOs of different industries. A consistent theme they have all shared has been the positive value of training your team. The industry and sector are irrelevant. The quality of the team's training consistently mirrors the bottom line and success of the organization. What I didn't understand was why the fitness world treated training and education as an elective.

After attending my first industry conference, I learned the value of continuing my education. I immediately saw the benefit in my paycheck. As a free-lancer, I observed the training protocol used by some of the big-box gyms. The new hire would shadow or follow along with a seasoned trainer for a few days. Twenty to forty hours of watching and they were off on their own. I doubted if this included any formal review or exam to prove competency afterward. There was not a standard used for the explanation of exercises or program design.

The fitness world used the law of survival to build their staffs. If you wanted to make it as a trainer, either look at the role or spend your free time studying. Most opted for the former. Prior to 2000, a few catapulted to the top of the industry because they saw the value in embracing both attributes. As social media has grown, the overall quality of training has improved. I cite entertainment and society's addiction to digital technology playing a heavy role, but the quality of training has moved in a positive direction. The fitness industry still trails most industries in the quality of their training of their staff.

I have observed a negative trend in the fitness, strength, and conditioning world. As we have shifted toward a world that social media plays a large role within, where trustworthiness is displayed by "Likes" and shares, there's been a transition to how someone looks from what they know. Your ability to entertain or impress others online has surpassed the desire to inspire and help others. That's a trend I don't recommend you follow. The role of a coach is a role of servitude, and I strongly urge you to resist this temptation and keep your objective as a teacher and leader in the fitness industry.

There's a common opening remark by presenters at conferences that the attendees should applaud themselves for being in attendance. "By being in attendance this weekend, consider yourself in the top 10% of the industry," is a common opening statement. I'm not sure if they truly mean this or if this is a tactic to befriend their audience. It was at one of these conferences that the void in staff training became very apparent to me. A well-recognized presenter with over forty years of experience as a gym owner and business consultant shared a story about one of his coaches. In the story, he was training on his gym floor when he came across a female member. He observed she was using a load that appeared too light. He quickly suggested that she use a heavier weight. She took his suggestion, increased the load, and continued training. After watching how easily the woman made the change, he sought her trainer and fired him. His reasoning was that the coach was not doing his job of challenging the client. My immediate thought was, what if the coach thought he was? What if the coach was the by-product of a poor training program and didn't know any better? As Robert Iger, past chair and CEO of the Walt Disney Company, wrote in his book, *The Ride of a Lifetime*, "Strong leadership embodies the fair and decent treatment of people. Empathy is essential, as is accessibility. People committing honest mistakes deserve second chances, and judging people too harshly generates fear and anxiety, which discourage communication and innovation. Nothing is worse to an organization than a culture of fear." [1]

The importance of training and counseling others goes back hundreds of years.

"Plans fail for lack of counsel, but with many advisors they succeed."

PROVERBS 15:22 (NIV)

One of the best examples of leadership in the face of judging the mistakes of others was typified by Abraham Lincoln. At the conclusion of the Civil War, he wanted to promote the overall healing the country needed to move forward. As Pulitzer Prize winner, Doris Kearns Goodwin, wrote in *Leadership in Turbulent Times*, "Enough lives have been sacrificed. We must extinguish our resentment if we expect harmony and union."[2] Confederate officers could return to their farms and plantations without repercussion from their position in the war.

Organizations are always looking for an edge. Thirty years ago, the competitive edge for many gyms was the equipment. As the industry grew and the recipe for results shifted toward the quality of coaching and less on the equipment, the difference between the industry leaders and the rest has been the education and training of the staff. One of the first organizations that I observed who embraced this was the Equinox Fitness organization. Equinox incentivized the staff with pay increases based upon education. They offered employees to earn accredited certifications and in return receive compensation increases. They also created an in-house staff of educators whose sole purpose was to gather education from third party education providers and then teach the staff. That model became an enormous influence on my role at the studio.

Inspired by the Equinox Group, I adopted a protocol of making continuing education readily available for my staff. I created an annual calendar of education. Twice a year, I would host an in-house summit for my coaches. This would be a half-day of exercise review, program design, and role playing among the coaches. We used case scenarios and discussed, as a group, best practices. It's a relaxed environment with any question up for discussion. We provide lunch for all the attendees. Everyone has the chance to teach and share. These summits serve as an opportunity for the less experienced coaches to learn and to build camaraderie among the team.

Once a year, we invite an outside education provider to work with the team for a day. My job is to vet the presenter, gather recommendations from fellow gym owners, and make sure they aligned with the training philosophy of the studio. I select topics and modalities unfamiliar to me. This provided the opportunity for us to learn together as a team.

Annually, the studio pays for the coaches to attend a conference. The Perform Better Functional Training Summit and the NSCA annual conference are a couple of examples. The coaches receive admission to the event, two nights at the sponsored hotel, and meals. These events not only serve as an opportunity to learn but also as a reward. It's important to surround your team with people from within their industry looking to improve. It's beneficial to get outside the walls of the studio and to learn in an unfamiliar environment. These events have elevated the overall quality of coaching in the industry.

PARADIGM 23

The efforts spent to you prepare and inspire your team will be reflective in your company's financial bottom line. Investment in your employees is a form of investment within your organization.

In 1991, when I began my journey as a coach, there was limited education available. As we come out of the temporary suspension of live events because of the global pandemic, and promoters host live events again, if you chose, you could attend an educational event every weekend of the year. Choosing which event to invest your educational dollars and time can be like attempting to take a drink from a firehose. As a leader for your team, you can help guide them to which option most affects both the welfare of your studio and also their career. An example of how I made the wrong decision happened to me immediately prior to opening my studio.

As I was outlining the format for my semi-private training model, I was deciding on what core equipment I would use. I narrowed it down to kettlebells, suspension trainers, and sandbags. I had been using each of these products with success with my private training clients and determined they would transfer over well to small-group training in a HIIT workout. This equipment had also proven to be durable and a smart investment, as I also had to consider cost. I began looking for any education or workshops available to further my competence using the tools. There was a single day workshop that ran with a local state clinic in California sponsored by the NSCA available. The organization administering the workshop was a manufacturer of a sandbag I was contemplating using at the studio. They slated for the workshop to last eight hours. After the opening remarks from the instructor, and approximately an hour of exercise discussion, the workshop shifted to a pitch on how to purchase the bags and how many you should have. They had allotted two hours for instruction and six hours for sales. The equipment provider had developed minimal education or training protocols for the sandbags. This upset me because I had spent the cost of airfare, hotel, and time away from my family on a weekend to attend a sales pitch. My error in judgment was based upon the assumption that the NSCA had vetted the education provider. I later learned they had spent their efforts scrutinizing presenters for their events and minimal time for pre- and post-event presenters. Experiences such as that can put a dark cloud over continuing education. As a leader for your team, you can avoid your coaches from having poor experiences in their learning journey. Attending poorly run educational events can leave a coach with the incorrect feeling that they have nothing else to learn. That can affect their career trajectory.

Gyms can take on the culture of a hair salon, if not closely monitored. It's commonplace in the salon industry to operate using independent contractors or free-lancers for staff. The stylist pays rent for their chair and may run their business within the walls of the salon. This nullifies the chance of creating a team environment or unified front among the staff. Each stylist or colorist can have a different approach on how to perform their job. Many strive to separate themselves from their contemporaries. There isn't a benefit to converting to a unified front. That can be troublesome in a training gym. Trainer A instructs a member how to perform an exercise. On the member's next visit, she works with another trainer, Trainer B. Trainer B teaches the same exercises completely different. The member experiences confusion and frustration. The training objective has shifted from learning the skill to trying to please the coach. If you take control of the education of your team, you minimize these scenarios and create a more standard language of coaching. You also ensure the quality of coaching and instruction used within your gym. Using the Starbucks franchise as an example, each location has the same way of preparing over 800 varieties of beverages.

When developing your staff, you should not take any assumptions about what they know and understand. Unless you have taken the time and effort to show them the skill, assume they do not understand it. In April 2018, they selected me to join the NSCA job task committee. The job of the committee was to audit the NSCA certified personal trainer exam and confirm that upon passing the exam, the participant attained competency in the tasks required for the job. This committee consisted of various gym owners throughout the USA. Wellness facilities, recreation centers, sports performance training enters, large box facilities, and boutique studios were all represented. There was substantial debate with the outcome that passing the exam confirmed proficiency at an entry level. What you should recognize is that if you are marketing high quality or "expert" coaching, an entry level staff member will not thrive.

Founders of law firms will tell you that an attorney who has completed law school and has passed the state required bar exam to practice law still requires months of training for skills such as writing motions and consulting clients. The measure of training and teaching an employee starts the action of true learning. This includes making mistakes and errors and then learning from them. As Daniel Coyle shares in *The Talent Code*, "The system of deep practice is where greatness and wisdom are created." You want to allow your employees to learn by constantly adjusting. The operator should look upon a new hire with the same eyes a mother has watching her toddler learn to walk. Falling and stumbling are the steps of learning how to walk. You want to create the environment where it's safe to fall down or take a misstep. The understanding is that they are learning. Mistakes and error provide a backdrop for learning for the novice coach.

Along with training your staff, you should also inspire your people. Jack Welch, former chair and CEO of GE, once said that a CEO should consider themselves the chief energy officer. "Everything rises and falls on leadership. If a team has leadership, that is always improving and inspiring them, that team reaches their highest level. Positive energy is contagious, and it's the job of leadership to instill an ethos of constantly improving in a positive environment."[3] A coach is a teacher and must embrace a spirit of servitude. Don't minimize the impact and influence that a coach can have on someone's life. Along with teaching a new coach how to perform a specific drill, there should be guidance on how to motivate others.

SPEAK THE SAME LANGUAGE

Everything in the exercise world is not black and white. There is a lot of gray. Different interpretations and opposing philosophies are part of strength and conditioning. It's not uncommon for experts to reference things using different terms. One of my earliest experiences was listening to a presenter at a conference discuss his approach to strengthen the posterior chain of the body. He used acronyms throughout his presentation that I was not familiar with. I can remember leaving frustrated. This validates the importance of why you should review any exercise you expect a fellow coach to administer. That involves an investment of time. The language of coaching is diverse and constantly growing. It's an error in management to assume that everyone will use the same reference points. The only way you can confirm this is by orienting and teaching your team exactly how you want something instructed. The Wizard of Westwood himself, UCLA basketball coach John Wooden, left nothing to be assumed. His choreographed practices are legendary and well documented. An example is how he reviewed the most mundane task to make sure everyone was on the same page. He started this system every season on the first day of practice. He would start by demonstrating how to put on your sock and sneaker. Legendary Hall of Fame player Bill Walton talks about how on his first day of practice, coach Wooden got everyone in a circle and started his lesson. Walton, the country's top-recruited player that year, thought "WHAT!!!???!!! We're top players! We don't need this!" But learning to tie shoes properly was vital to Wooden. "Make sure your heel is full seated in the sock's heel; run your hand over the toes and smooth out any bumpy areas."[4] Then he showed each player how to lace his shoes and tie them snugly, so there was no room for the shoe to rub or the sock to bunch up. It meant star players would never get a blister, which would keep them from playing. The team can't be its best unless everyone's able to play. If legendary coach Wooden took the time to explain how to put your socks on, don't you think you should discuss how to perform an Olympic lift or kettlebell swing with your coaches?

A common trait among good leaders is that they become

comfortable repeating themselves. Good leaders are comfortable repeating and reminding their team of objectives, goals, and core values. Good leaders seize this as part of their job. The consistent voice from leadership allows everyone to row the boat in the same direction. I didn't always understand this. In the early days of opening the studio, I considered the echoing coaching technique as a waste of time. I would question the quality of the hire when rehashing something shared prior. I had a moment of clarity when I realized people hear things at different times. Think about a lesson that someone attempted to teach you early on, that finally became understood years down the road. I also came to understand that when dealing with more than two people, you will repeat the same statement, but to another person. If you take a top view of teaching, you will come to admire the value of teaching fundamentals. As a trainer, you should become comfortable repeating yourself. You understand that learning is a process. Coaches of sports teams understand that the team they have on the first day of practice will become a different group by season's end. You aren't repeating, but reinforcing, what needs to be understood.

We all want to be accepted. As a trainer, you are working to help someone achieve a goal. Helping someone to achieve what they set out to capture is the ultimate way to reach buy-in. Leading and supporting your team so that they can be successful in helping others is not only morally good, but a solid business model. Accept a role of mentoring and teaching those that work for you and your bottom line will reap the benefits. John Maxwell wrote in his book, *The 21 Irrefutable Laws of Leadership*:

"Many people view leadership the same way they view success, hoping to go as far as they can, to climb the ladder, to achieve the highest position possible for their talent. But contrary to conventional thinking, I believe the bottom line in leadership isn't how far we advance ourselves, but how far we advance others."

Prior to opening my studio, while I was subletting floor space from a dance studio, I can remember a conversation with the studio owner that clarified the importance of leadership within your business. The studio owner had just returned from a weekend of judging at a state ballroom dancing competition. He joked that he always returns from these trips, hoping everything is okay with his business when he opens. He then shared that he didn't want employees who he had to "babysit." His plan was to hire instructors and have them work diligently and focused, with no guidance or mentoring. In his five years of being open, he was never profitable and closed six months after we had this discussion. In this scenario, the studio owner did not understand his role as a leader and didn't value mentorship.

Companies are always looking for an edge. You're reading this book right now to gain insight that may help you become better. Organizations invest in technology with aspirations that it will improve their efficiency. Marketing companies fill social media with advertisements claiming to super charge their sales funnel with a new campaign. Gyms will hire consultants to come in and evaluate, with hopes they will provide the few fixes they need. I'm not denying that all of those can help, but to be successful, your team will need more. Your studio needs leadership. John Maxwell wrote in *A Leader's Heart*:

"Personnel determine the potential of the team.

Vision determines the direction of the team.

Work ethic determines the preparation of the team.

Leadership determines the success of the team."

Systems allow your gym to operate efficiently. Systems do not allow you to run things void of leadership. To scale your business, you need to build a team. You want to attract good people. There is an attraction between good people to good leadership. As a leader, you will want results. Before you achieve those results, focus on becoming a good leader. "Being" will proceed "doing."

> ## PARADIGM 24
>
> All organizations require leadership. Do not expect your team to be led by their own ambition and discipline. As the owner of your business, you have the responsibility to lead.

PROVIDE CONSTANT FEEDBACK

Poor management is providing feedback only when there is a problem. That's a pigeon manager. A pigeon manager flies, drops waste all over everything, and leaves as fast as they flew in. Everyone thrives on feedback. A sign of maturity as a coach is when you attain enough confidence that you can ask people how they feel. It does not intimidate you to ask, and you are eager to adjust things if needed. As you gain more experience, your confidence improves, which aids communication. I can say the same when working with your team.

You should constantly check in with your team. Provide them feedback when things are going well and guide them when something needs adjusting. Don't expect them to come to you. One-on-ones with staff are a valuable tool and do not need to be formal. Taking the time to tell someone they are doing a good job is just as valuable as critiques of things they need to improve on. The key is that they should have a balance. It's your job to make sure it gets done. Jack Welch, of GE, famously said that 50% of employees don't know if they are doing a good job. You want feedback built upon candor and honesty, not fluff. Your goal is to make the person better. If you are transparent in your objectives, then your team should welcome the feedback.

Every team member should have an annual review. This process is a formal review which allows you to document their performance and then share with the team member. It should follow a standard format used by everyone. Attendance, behavior, and achieved goals are common areas discussed. Reviews are a good time to discuss professional and personal goals with your team. You want to play a role in helping your team stay accountable. Annual reviews take a big picture perspective when compared to the daily, weekly, and monthly informal one-on-ones. They should reinforce why you hired the person and if they are fulfilling their role as expected. Use this time to discuss bonuses and pay increases. Approach these reviews as an opportunity to help your team improve. Don't avoid discussing their areas of weakness. The key is to provide feedback on how they can improve. Don't point out a problem unless you can provide a solution.

As an owner and manager, understand that people outgrow roles. In many start-ups, the team that starts out on the journey is not typically the team you bring to the game. This was a growth step in my personal development as a leader when I grasped staff will come and go. As your studio matures, so do you as an operator and your ability to hire. The skill set and traits you thought were suffice for a job may no longer be adequate. From the perspective of the team member, it is not uncommon for employees to experience a life change during their time with you and then decide they want a career in a different industry. The fitness industry attracts people who enjoy training and being in the gym. Coaches who stay in the industry understand that they have undertaken a job of servitude. A good coach enjoys serving others. This required trait weeds people out of the industry.

When people decide to move on from your employment,

remember to treat them with dignity. There is a professional way to end a business relationship. Your team observes how you treat other employees in these situations. If they give you notice, then agree on a last day, discuss your policy on providing references and wish them well. Do not look at their position as a void you have to fill, but a past investment of time and service they provided you.

A few years after opening, I started to conduct exit interviews with all employees who gave notice and moved on from the studio. The purpose of exit interviews is to gain feedback and insight so that you can make improvements. The aim is to reduce turnover and improve on keeping staff. This insight can be shocking and bothersome. As an operator, you need to be mentally prepared and go into these with an open mind. People who don't have an invested interest in your company tend to be brutally honest. I can remember when one of my team members told me it bothered him when I passed him up for more training hours. His attitude soon soured, and he started looking for another job soon after. Reflecting on that situation, I learned to consider everyone's feelings when I give promotions or upward opportunities. A brief 5-minute discussion in private can go a long way in softening the blow to someone's psyche.

PARADIGM 25

A core foundation of providing feedback is to help make someone better. Placing heavy emphasis on the current dilemma is a way to stalling performance. Instead, focus on how they can better perform in future and not how they made mistakes in the past.

LEADING DURING A GLOBAL PANDEMIC

The military routinely performs exercises or war games to see the effects of war times and to test resources. It's a time to challenge strategies and affirm suggested outcomes. I don't believe many in the fitness industry could have predicted the global pandemic of 2020. Being forced through government mandates to shelter in place and close created devastating effects in the fitness industry, and the ripples are still playing out years later. Case study review and analysis is part of the process in working toward your master's degree in business. With that in mind, here is a chronological review of how I operated the studio during the pandemic.

February 2020- Concerns are rising domestically about COVID-19. State and Federal governments presented mixed messages in the media. Our studio experienced a drop-off in attendance from member anxiety.

March 16, 2020- The state of Nevada documents its first death from COVID-19. At 5:00 PM, Governor Steve Sisolak addressed the state in a live press conference from the Grant Sawyer Building in Las Vegas. The state of California closed nonessential businesses the week prior, and it was largely rumored that the state of Nevada would soon follow. During the eighteen-minute press conference, the governor mandated the closure of all nonessential businesses by midnight of the following day. That included casinos. In the state of Nevada, gaming and tourism are one of the largest generators of revenue. I locked up the studio and headed home that evening to think about my options. My phone began beeping with text messages from my members.

I considered keeping the studio open for private training only, allowing only two trainers in the studio at a time. This would limit the risk of spreading the virus. Our studio provides small-group training, with groups up to a maximum of six people, and private one-on-one training. After forty-eight hours of deliberation, I determined it was in my immediate best interest to comply and completely close the studio and suspend all live training. I believe in following the rules of safety and didn't want to create an image that I was ignoring what the science was telling us at that time. I drafted and sent out an email for my members explaining that I would open on the following Monday to allow them to stop by the studio to pick up and lease equipment for training at home. My priority was to determine how could I generate cash flow while being closed. Renting equipment was a simple option. Re-purposing equipment that was going to sit unused, for an unknown amount of time, was a quick way to create some cash flow.

My next step was to create a schedule of workouts the members could follow virtually. I froze every current membership. These were unprecedented times. Anxiety was high because of the unknown. I knew my members would remember down the road the way I treated them during the stressful times. We show character during the most challenging of times. Unlike many of my competitors, I froze and suspended all current memberships and then offered each member the opportunity to opt into a separate membership during this time. I considered it unethical to continue charging my members for a membership which they had to enter the studio. Any coach with years of experience will agree that training live is different and a service of higher regard than training someone via online or virtually. How could I offer them a virtual service and charge the equivalent fee of training them in person? That is not what they agreed to in their membership agreement. When each member inquired about my services, I did not discuss virtual training. I didn't feel that switching the service of live training to virtual and offering it as equal in value was ethical. I believed that offering a smaller fee for virtual training would enhance the value of training at the studio once we could reopen.

PARADIGM 26

True character is displayed not during moments of prosperity but during times of stress and disorder.

March 21, 2020- The next step was to contact my team. I kept my operation's assistant on to assist with managing the new billing and operations of the virtual setup. I furloughed my coaches until further notice. Calling each of them with the news was one of the hardest things I've had to do since opening the studio. My initial feeling was that I was letting them down. The governor announced we would have to close for thirty days. That would eventually lead to two months. I knew it was in the best interest for everyone, for me to work toward maintaining a business for them to return to. In situations like this, I understood I should keep the dialogue brief and be honest.

Operating the studio has two big expenses: payroll and the lease. Furloughing, the coaches cut the payroll expense. The hard cost of the lease is something I had to address. I knew cash preservation was key. I immediately contacted my landlord and asked for the suspension of two months' rent that I could pay over the remaining months of my lease. To my benefit, I had nine months remaining on my lease. That minimized my liabilities if the worst-case scenario was to close. This arrangement worked for my landlord because he didn't have to wait long for repayment. He agreed to the terms.

I had a credit line with my bank. I immediately withdrew from the credit line and deposited a half month's revenue into my account for capital reserves. Up to this point, I maintained a month's worth of cash in the bank for capital reserve. The gold standard was to keep three months. Looking back, we were just getting our flywheel going. In the first three years of operating the studio, I was quick to reinvest back into the business. I should have put more capital aside. The pandemic is a once in a generational event, but as an owner, you should always work on building capital reserves. That is a painful lesson I learned.

March 23, 2020- I offered virtual training sessions. I am the sole coach, so I am forced to administer the workouts three times daily, six days a week. The members followed along with me in live time. I scaled the sessions, working with more people at once, but I sacrifice personalized attention for correcting and critiquing. Coaching adjustments and feedback are cornerstones of what my members have grown to expect, but I have no other option. A third of my members participated in the new format. At fifty years of age and twenty-nine years of training people, I have lived by the mantra that it's not what I can do, but what I can teach that matters. I will have to adjust that stance for the next couple of months, as it will be what I can do and show that matters.

The toll of conducting three workouts daily, six days a week, is brutal. After two weeks, my knees and back have chronic soreness. My goal is to keep it going until I get a feel for when we'll be able to reopen. Once we're within a couple of weeks, I can bring my coaches back to assist with the workload. Right now, I must hunker down and preserve cash.

March 27, 2020- Congress signs into effect the Coronavirus Aid, Relief and Economic Security (CARES) act. This act included The Paycheck Protection Program (PPP) which will provide loans to small business which enabled them to bring back staff. There are parameters which transform the loan into a forgivable grant if I spend most of the capital on payroll. That amount eventually changed from 75% to 60%. The first round of funding went fast, and I didn't make the cut. I have relationships with two banks. One is a large national bank, and the other is a local institution. The larger bank catered to their larger customers. This was scrutinized by the media later. It was the small local bank that qualified me for PPP and provided funding. The PPP loan threw me a lifeline. That money allowed me to bring two of my coaches back and provided me relief for payroll and money toward my lease. Things were turning.

April 1, 2020- Governor Sisolak extended the closure date for nonessential businesses until April 30th. I wrote several letters to his office asking that they consider opening fitness facilities in a capacity-based manner. I feared getting grouped with the larger big-box gyms. There is a growing community of micro-gyms (gyms under 10,000 square feet) that were being overlooked. At peak times, my studio has eleven people inside. A small group has a maximum size of six people. We can also have two coaches conducting private training. That's eight members and three coaches in 2,400 square feet. That provides approximately 200 square feet per person. My plan on how to adjust to the current crisis once we may reopen was to lower the small-group training size down from six to four people to allow for better social distancing. I purchased an air purifier that sanitized the air. Upon entering the studio, every person had to use the hand-free sanitizers mounted on the walls. Members did not share equipment, and we sanitized the equipment after every usage. We purchased ultra-violet light sanitizers to help expedite the cleaning. The smaller size of the studio allowed me to quickly implement these changes. We could administer quality coaching without sacrificing the safety of our members. I contacted the local FOX news outlet and was featured, showing the steps we were taking to keep our members safe.

Coverage from local Fox news outlet prior to re-opening during the pandemic.

April 24, 2020- After five weeks of the statewide closure, I hired an attorney. I needed legal advice. I was considering breaking the mandate and prematurely re-opening. It helped that she was a member of the studio. I didn't have to explain the dynamic and culture of the studio. She was aware and had observed and experienced the safety and professionalism of my team. I was weighing the risk versus the reward of re-opening. Up to this point, the governor had threatened fines and the suspension of business licenses if you violated the mandate and opened. I didn't have an issue complying with the mandate. The problem I had was that they had changed the date for re-opening twice and would not provide clear dates for re-opening. They granted me PPP, which would become a loan, if not used for payroll. Under the current conditions, the lifeline would become a liability, not a lifeline, as it was. The fitness industry is void of representation with our governor. He categorizes all gyms, fitness facilities, and studios together. I received no response from the emails I sent to his office.

I wanted to get a pulse on the emotions of my members. It didn't matter if I decided to reopen if no one felt safe to come in. I sent out a survey to all the members. I mapped out how we would conduct training under the current conditions. This included the coaches wearing masks, social distancing, no shared equipment, and the usage of an air filtration unit. 80% responded that they felt safe and would come back immediately.

May 4, 2020- I could see light at the end of the tunnel. The fourteen-day daily infection and death rates are dropping within the state. To satisfy the conditions of PPP, I brought my coaches back in to administer the virtual training sessions. I needed to get my staff prepared for re-opening. That included getting my coaches off the couch and back into form. They are working only part time, but my goal was to re-ignite our sense of working as a team again. You cannot turn on culture like a faucet. The pandemic created a sense of survival. I needed to engage with my team to have them working as a unit, as in the past. They performed the training sessions over Zoom, but I could see the spark back in their eyes as they engaged with our members. Coaching is an art, and I had to re-engage the skill they had left dormant for six weeks.

May 25, 2020- After nine weeks of being closed, I reopened the studio. Things were different. We had 65% of our base come back immediately. An additional 10% would come back within sixty days. There are 15% of our members who cited concerns about the pandemic and terminated their membership and did not return. In past years, June and July are typically flat months. Kids get out of school and it's vacation season. Las Vegas has mild winters, but intense summers. Temperatures north of 105 degrees have a way of demotivating people and crushing the normal walk-in traffic experienced throughout the rest of the year. We typically don't have attrition, but growth is stagnant. In contrast to past years though, because of pent up demand and people avoiding the heavily populated big-box gyms, we experience a surge of new members in the summer months.

The governor did not allow gyms to reopen. I weighed the revenue I was losing weekly and decided to take the risk of being fined. Lucky to have law enforcement officers as members, they informed me that the state didn't have adequate staff to enforce the mandate. The only shops being cited were businesses that had complaints called in. Our members appreciated all the precautions that we had taken, so I didn't have those worries. One week later, the governor would allow gyms to reopen, effective June first.

November 9, 2020- Five months after re-opening our studio, we returned to pre-pandemic numbers. We would still have daily obstacles to overcome, like all small businesses, but the worst was behind us. I could feel the sun coming out. My mind could finally shift from the fight-or-flight state it had been in for the past five months. Similar to life, business runs in seasons. The dark winter of the pandemic was behind us, for now.

Reflecting on 2020, I experienced my biggest window of growth as a leader. There was no playbook or past case scenario to draw guidance from. I had to evaluate situations weekly, daily, and sometimes by the hour. What I learned is that no one knows your business better than you. You understand the needs of your team and your consumer. No one can tell you what's in your best interest. You determine that. Everyone has a different level of risk tolerance. The ability to stay calm in turbulent situations and think risk versus benefit can be one of the most valuable assets for any leader. In hindsight, I believe that your biggest moments in business will come during your most challenging of times.

> ## PARADIGM 27
> Regardless of what the experts say, never ignore what you experience and observe with your own eyes within your business. Personal experiences are the best form of data you can collect.

YOUR JOB AS A LEADER

In the fitness world, a common discussion is how to select the appropriate tool for the client, whether it be a barbell, kettlebell, or suspension trainer, and how to use it. For your team to execute their tasks effectively, they are going to need the tools. It's your job as a leader to insure they have the tools and proper skills. John C. Maxwell, in his book *The Maxwell Leadership Bible*, lists the gifts that a leader should give their team:

"I must CARE for them (Communication, Affirmation, Recognition, and Example)

I must work on their weaknesses but work out their strengths.
I must give them myself (time, energy, focus).
I must become a resource person (atmosphere, training, support, tools).
I must make expectations clear.
I must eliminate unnecessary burdens.
I must catch them doing something good, then reward them for it."[5]

Leadership is not an option when opening a studio. It must be present, or you will fail. It's a skill that is learned. Take the time to focus on becoming better, and you will. It cannot be a trait you turn off and on. Leadership is something that never turns off. All business owners are driven to want results. Your ability to lead will directly affect those results. Lead by doing, not by saying. Strive to improve your character and your leadership skills will improve as a by-product. Good leadership attracts good people. Your team will not care what you know until they know you care about them.

You should have a unique relationship with each member of your team. As your business grows and matures and you take on more administrative responsibility, you may choose to take yourself from the training floor, but you shouldn't remove your presence. Your people need to feel connected to you. They will model your behavior and that's good for molding a positive culture. People will do what they see, not what they hear. The example you put forth is vital for success.

Take the 80/20 approach and, if possible, have them spend 80% of their time performing tasks that cater to their strengths. Everyone has a superpower. A skill that they excel at. Assign duties that position people to optimize their superpower. This doesn't mean you should ignore areas of weakness. Help them improve on their weaknesses and flaws. This is when humility can aid a leader. Reflect on when you started as a coach, and the mistakes that occurred along your journey.

In the early days of the studio, I frequently fought for time. I learned how to better manage my time, but that alone did not trickle over to better rapport with my team. I had to schedule time in my schedule to be available for my team. I used this time to talk about personal issues, family, and other interests they may have. Ten minutes of talk can show someone that you care about the job they do and the person who they are.

CHAPTER 9

IN CONCLUSION

SUCCESSFULLY OPERATING a boutique studio is a skill I undervalued prior to opening. I quickly realized that my team's and my success teetered on how well I could quickly learn and make corrections. Running a successful small business is built on the foundation of perseverance, challenging work, and constant learning. You don't only get points for showing up, but also for improving along the way. The good news is that you can get better if you choose to. Entrepreneurship is one of the most challenging, but rewarding, experiences you can have. Understand that you will make mistakes along the way. You're never fully prepared. As you embark on your journey, don't be embarrassed to ask for help from others. Make an impact by making things better and you will succeed.

To achieve success, you must first define what that means. The definition of success is unique to each of us. Spend the necessary valuable time to reflect on the questions posed in this book. As Jim Rohn once said, "Success leaves clues." Answer those questions and then you can determine who you wish to serve. Your blueprint is drawn based upon those questions you have learned how to ask. Now, all you must do is create and build your masterpiece. Good luck!

RESOURCES

Certifications

National Strength and Conditioning Association (NSCA) www.nsca.com

American Council of Exercise (ACE) www.acefitness.org

American College of Sports Medicine (ACSM) www.acsm.org

The National Academy of Sports Medicine (NASM) www.nasm.org

StrongFirst www.strongfirst.com

Certified Functional Strength Coach (CFSC) www.certifiedfsc.com

Functional Movement Systems (FMS) www.functional-movement.com

Precision Nutrition www.Precisionnutrition.com

Education Providers

National Strength and Conditioning Association (NSCA) www.nsca.com

IDEA Health and Fitness Association www.ideafit.com

Perform Better www.Performbetter.com

Recommended Reading

The E-Myth by Michael E. Gerber

The Effective Executive by Peter F. Drucker

The Lean Startup by Eric Ries

MindSet The New Psychology of Success by Carol S. Dweck, Ph.D.

High Output Management by Andrew S. Grove

The Checklist Manifesto by Atul Gawande

Crossing the Chasm by Geoffrey A. Moore

Influence The Psychology of Persuasion by Dr. Robert B. Cialdini, Ph.D.

Atomic Habits by James Clear

Hooked: How to Build Habit-Forming Products by Nir Eyal with Ryan Hoover

The Purple Cow by Seth Godin

The 21 Irrefutable Laws of Leadership by Dr. John C. Maxwell

The Maxwell Leadership Bible: Lesson in Leadership from the Word of God by Dr. John C. Maxwell 2002, 2007

Leadership in Turbulent Times by Doris Kearns Goodwin

Team of Teams by General Stanley McChrystal

Setting the Table by Danny Meyer

Built from Scratch by Bernie Marcus and Arthur Blank

NOTES

1. MY PERSPECTIVE

1. Int J Sports Phys Ther. 2012 Apr; 7(2): 226–241. THE EFFECTIVENESS OF RESISTANCE TRAINING USING UNSTABLE SURFACES AND DEVICES FOR REHABILITATION
David Behm, PhD[1] and Juan Carlos Colado, PhD[2]
2. The Psychology of Money, Timeless Lessons on Wealth, Greed, and Happiness by Morgan Housel
3. Clance, P. R. and Imes, S. A (1978). The imposter phenomenon in high achieving women: Dynamics and therapeutic intervention. Psychotherapy: Theory, Research & Practice, Vol 15(3), 241-247.
4. *Atomic Habits* by James Clear

2. WHO AM I GOING TO TRAIN?

1. Source: Bureau of Labor Statistics, Business Employment Dynamics.
2. Med Sci Sports Exerc 1996 Oct;28(10):1327-30. doi: 10.1097/00005768-199610000-00018
3. Exerc Sport Sci Rev. 2008 Apr;36(2):58-63. doi: 10.1097/JES.0b013e318168ec1f
4. Gym memberships in the U.S. 2000-2017 | Statista
5. Crossing the Chasm, 3rd Edition: Marketing and Selling Disruptive Products to Mainstream Customers by Geoffrey Moore
6. The Tim Ferriss Show Transcripts: Eric Schmidt (#367) – The Blog of Author Tim Ferriss
7. (271) Steve Jobs Secrets of Life - YouTube

3. SETTING UP THE FOUNDATION

1. 3 Time-Management Tips From Twitter and Square CEO Jack Dorsey | Inc.com
2. Meyer, D. E., Evans, J. E., Lauber, E. J., Gmeindl, L., Rubinstein, J., Junck, L., & Koeppe, R. A. (1998). The role of dorsolateral prefrontal cortex for executive cognitive processes in task switching. Journal of Cognitive Neuroscience, 1998, Vol. 10.
   Meyer, D. E., Evans, J. E., Lauber, E. J., Rubinstein, J., Gmeindl, L.,

Junck, L., & Koeppe, R. A. (1997). Activation of brain mechanisms for executive mental processes in cognitive task switching. Journal of Cognitive Neuroscience, 1997, Vol. 9.

> http://www.apa.org/research/action/multitask.aspx

3. Website: The American Presidency Project, Speech delivered by: Dwight D. Eisenhower, Speech number: 204, Title: Address at the Second Assembly of the World Council of Churches, Location: Evanston, Illinois, Date: August 19, 1954, Website description: The American Presidency Project was established in 1999 as a collaboration between John T. Woolley and Gerhard Peters at the University of California, Santa Barbara. Archives contain 104,855 documents related to the study of the Presidency. (Accessed presidency.ucsb.edu on May 8, 2014) link
4. HBR Ideacast 802- The Rise and Fall of Carlos Ghosn
5. https://www.forbes.com/sites/nishacharya/2015/05/19/jack-welch-be-the-chief-meaning-officer/?sh=766405803441

4. MONDAYS ARE FOR MARKETING

1. https://kk.org/thetechnium/1000-true-fans/
2. Positioning: How to be Seen and Heard in the Overcrowded Marketplace by Al Ries and Jack Trout
3. https://logos.fandom.com/wiki/Apple
4. *Hooked: How to Build Habit-Forming Products* by Nir Eyal
5. https://www.domo.com/assets/downloads/18_domo_data-never-sleeps-6+verticals.pdf

5. BY THE NUMBERS

1. https://info.bloomintelligence.com/hubfs/Miscellaneous%20Downloads/Restaurant%20Benchmarks.pdf

6. OPERATIONS- THE REALITY IS MESSY AND COMPLEX

1. *The Checklist Manifesto*, Atul Gawande, chapter three pg.49
2. https://www.sba.gov/blog/franchise-fees-why-do-you-pay-them-how-much-are-they
3. https://www.wired.com/2012/11/amy-cuddy-first-impressions/#:~:text=A%20strong%20handshake%20and%20assertive,psychologist%20Amy%20Cuddy%20explains%20why.
4. *Setting the Table: The Transforming Power of Hospitality in Business* by Danny Meyer

5. https://en.wikipedia.org/wiki/Greek_to_me
6. https://www.newsmax.com/FastFeatures/industries-nevada-economy/2015/04/14/id/638269/

7. HIRING YOUR TEAM

1. Traction: Get a Grip on Your Business by Gino Wickman

8. SKILL AND WILL

1. The Ride of a Lifetime, Prologue pg. XXii by Robert Iger
2. Leadership in Turbulent Times, pg. 363 by Doris Kearns Goodwin
3. *Winning* by Jack Welch and Suzy Welch
4. http://blog.damelionetwork.com/sports-motivational-speaker-bill-walton-learning-to-tie-shoes-was-john-wooden-success-lesson-for-life
5. The Maxwell Leadership Bible: Lesson in Leadership from the Word of God by Dr. John C. Maxwell 2002, 2007

I have drawn inspiration and been mentored by people whom I have never formally met. Jim Rohn inspired me to be a reader. It was his remarks that books are "bread for the head" and that "leaders are readers" that got me to pick up books once I was out of school, and has made reading part of my daily life. This habit has enriched my life, and I'm grateful for that.

Colin Powel taught me that people will follow what you do, not what you say. He was a great example of living with integrity. Thank you, sir.

I want to thank Jerry White. Jerry, you helped get me my first job as a personal trainer with Bally's Total Fitness. Until I met you, I never thought I could have a career as a personal trainer, which became the backdrop for this book.

Thank you, Steve Weinberger, Bev Francis, and Powerhouse Gym of Syosset, for providing my first home as a free-lance personal trainer. Powerhouse Gym was a great place for me to start my journey as a trainer and start working on my craft.

Thank you, Leora Blau, for saying the right words at the right time. Las Vegas was not on my radar as a home until you brought it up and said the words that gave me the confidence to move across country.

I watched Juan "JC" Santana present in 2000 at an IDEA conference and it changed my life. JC was the first educator that I observed that I felt I could relate with. Thanks, JC, for allowing your personality to come through when you present.

I want to thank Mike Boyle for his leadership in the strength and conditioning industry. Thank you, Mike, for always speaking with honesty, and your pragmatic approach. I resonated with you the first time I heard you speak, and twenty years later I still do.

I want to thank Alwyn Cosgrove for being an example for both a competent coach and business owner. Alwyn, many of today's successful gym owners are standing on your shoulders. I'm thankful for what you have contributed to personal training for the general population.

Thank you, Conrad Hibbert, Chris Poirier, and the Perform Better team for providing me the equipment to operate my studio. Conrad, I appreciate you always picking up the phone when I call. Chris, thank you for your efforts to organize quality educational events. The Perform Better educational events have been a large influence on me and my practice.

I want to thank my team at J & D Fitness Personal Training. This book is part of my maturation process of becoming a good leader for each of you. Thank you for allowing me to lead you.

Stacey Smekofske, thank you for being my editor and taking me on as a client and navigating me through this process. This has been very challenging and rewarding at the same time.

I want to thank my illustrator Morain An for creating a beautiful cover and helping to give a face to this book.

Dad, you were my first mentor. Thank you for the sacrifices you made for me. Much of my value system comes from your influence. At a time when personal training was not financially lucrative, you never deterred me from following my dream.

To my wife, Judy, thank you for pushing me to fulfill my potential. I could not do what I do without your consistent support. You were the first example of a professional trainer I got to observe every day.

I want to thank God, because without you, none of this is possible.

To every client that trusted me as a trainer, thank you. Each of you helped form a block in the foundation of my training career.

ABOUT THE AUTHOR

Douglas Sheppard is a certified personal trainer. He is the owner of J&D Fitness Personal Training Studio in Las Vegas, Nevada. He is a writer, public speaker, consultant, and coach with over 30 years of experience.

You can find out more about Doug at www.Janddfitness.com

www.ingramcontent.com/pod-product-compliance
Lightning Source LLC
Chambersburg PA
CBHW071314150726
47997CB00002B/473